Looking Back at a rather Warped but Wonderful Childhood

A.J. Mueller

Copyright © 2018 A.J. Mueller

All rights reserved.

Do not even think of plagiarizing anything from this manuscript, no one will ever believe you.

ISBN: 978-0-9970118-2-1

DEDICATION

To my lovely wife Marsha, to all of my children, my siblings, my family, my extended family, my dogs, my dog's extended families, my dog's extended family's families, my loyal readers (all three of you!), their extended families and all of those 'out there' that will buy this book and, of course, to your wonderful extended families who you should psychologically force to buy this book.

CONTENTS

	Introduction	Pg # 3
1	Get Out It's a BOMB!	Pg # 6
2	Home Sweet Home	Pg # 10
3	The Family Tree	Pg # 16
4	The Hamilton Years	Pg # 26
5	Sentenced to Rawdon	Pg # 32
6	The Westmount Years	Pg # 36
7	The Senneville Hillbillys	Pg # 45
8	Good Evening, American Style!	Pg # 62
9	New York, New York	Pg # 68
10	The Pot of Soup Theory	Pg # 73
11	The Way to Treat an Angry Bear!	Pg # 87
12	No Ticky, No Laundry	Pg # 92
13	I Can Fly, I Can Fly!	Pg # 95
14	Energy Conservation	Pg # 98
15	Dad, Duchess and Customs Officers	Pg # 103
16	The Orphanage	Pg # 109
	Epilogue	Pg # 112

INTRODUCTION

I have always been interested in personal history, hearing the individual recollections of days gone by is pretty cool. I often wonder, however, what really transpired, for recollections are but one person's interpretation of what they think actually took place, and history dictates, that this at times can be very far indeed from the actual occurrences of the time.

Childhood remembrances hold even greater intrigue to me for even though age and maturity may have set in at the time of the recollection, the actual recall of the circumstances can be somewhat tainted being based upon what was seen and heard through the eyes and ears of a non-sophisticated and very, very innocent child.

Please keep this in mind as you make your way through this book.

I have a good friend who graduated from college with a degree in psychology. He is now in the real estate business which I would imagine is a pretty good place to put some deep understanding of human behavior to good use. The real estate business is possibly even better and more satisfying than hanging a 'shingle' out as a psychologist. I say that because even he, after years and years of studying all things psychological, openly admits that trying to figure out exactly why someone acts the way they do is an exercise in futility. Trying to utilize that knowledge to actually effect a meaningful, beneficial change in that individual is an even greater waste of one's precious time, sometimes people are just really irretrievably 'screwed up'!

Do you ever wonder about your psychological makeup? You know, what made you who you are and why you carry out your life the way you do? This can be even more intriguing if you have blood brothers and sisters who came from the exact same surroundings and family upbringing, brothers and sisters who are very different than you in the way they act, react and handle life in general.

I certainly wonder about it, in fact I have wrestled with these questions for most of my time on earth. Now don't get me wrong, you won't find me sitting up all night in the dark, absolutely sleepless over this but it is a somewhat regular event in my life.

My brother George, God rest his soul, was a couple of years older than me, was brought up by our very same parents, in the very same house, and had the advantage of at least a few more years of family unit stability than did I. Many, many people when we were in our young adulthood thought that we looked and acted the same, in fact we would often be mistaken for each other. On the surface they would be correct, we did indeed share a desire for fast cars, fast females and life in the fast lane. But if one were to have got a glimpse into our minds they would have seen a huge difference. He chose a much different psychological path than did I, unfortunately, a dark well-trod pathway leading to his ultimate personal destruction, and this voluntary choice was his regardless of the many special 'breaks' during his so-called formative years. Why, what mental process took place that made his personal choices so different than mine? That is a great question and one which even more unfortunately will not be answered in this book. There are, however, many revelations contained in the following pages that may shed light on why I question our different behavior as well as my own social outcome. I often think that the path taken by my brother was actually the most logical one to have been taken by me.

I've never been accused of being really bizarre. I don't think that anyone out there considers me to be exceptionally strange or overly weird, I certainly do not. And I am certainly not some anti-social misfit. I do not regularly abuse alcohol, although I will openly admit to getting far-too-loose from its use on far-too-many occasions. Lucky for me when I do over-indulge, I tend to get more mellow and friendly, not nasty and vicious, sort of that not so subtle difference between the all-too-likable town drunk (like *Otis* on the Andy Griffith Show) and the all-too-easy to hate mean-spirited alcoholic (pick one, you certainly know a bunch!).

Additionally I do not now, nor have I ever, knowingly ingested recreational pharmaceuticals, and I do not have a police record. So there, when judged by most contemporary standards I am a relatively normal individual, whatever 'normal' actually is. What I find really strange is that I am so damned normal. If we apply contemporary thinking regarding one's upbringing and background on the final human product, I should be an absolute anti-social misfit and a total waste of a person. I, however, have managed to reach the ripe old age of 70 plus a few, and I am still staying 'in line'. I continue to blend in and actually, at least in my opinion, continue to contribute positively to society (this book may be an exception) without any conscious controls on my part, or external brain altering shockwave devices mandated by the courts or their agents for the safety of the general public.

My opinion that I should have been a real sick wacko is based on a number of things. Firstly, like far too many of the warped psycho serial-killer types, I too came from a broken home, well actually, it was a shattered home. Dad may have been one hell of a macho guy, but as a father he was severely challenged, in fact as close to a total failure at parenthood as one could possibly get. He most certainly was, at the very least, an excessive abuser of alcohol, tobacco, and firearms. I suspect that he also regularly used, and abused, a host of other questionable substances, including a number of humans. There were others as well who were around during my childhood years that were equally mentally distressing to me. For whatever the reasons may have been, there was always an abundance of truly weird, wild happenings involving and surrounding me as a little kid and up through when I was a teenager. When I say weird, I mean mentally agitating, highly questionable, weird things!

I have picked two stories to quickly illustrate what I mean, they are the first two stories in this book. Enjoy!

CHAPTER 1 - GET OUT.... IT'S A BOMB!

It was 1950 or 1951 and World War Two, which had ended a few years earlier, had been replaced with peace and tranquility, at least in the minds of most in the United States of America. After reading this, however, you may agree that some still lacked those post-war warm, fuzzy feelings of mental tranquility.

I recall being in that most formative period of five or six years old at the time and for whatever reasons found myself and some of my siblings at my grandparents house for the day. This was not all that unusual for we used to spend time there on a regular basis, it was a good experience most of the time. Grandpa was a most interesting guy and a very, very fascinating almost mind-captivating person to spend time with to say the least... as long as you were mentally prepared for imminent danger and the mini disasters which always seemed to follow him. Even at that tender age of five or six I could clearly see that semi-crazed look deep in his eyes regardless of his and Grandma's constant attempts at psychologically disguising him as a lay-back 'normal' 'Gramps' type. They certainly did not fool me and as the years passed to say that my suspicions were confirmed would be somewhat of a gross understatement. Fortunately for you, my loyal readers, Grandpa and his dramatic personal effect on my mushrooming psychological makeup, will be a recurring figure in this book, sort of like 'Mr. Celophaneman' in the musical *Chicago*.

Any effort by me to define just how and why I turned out the way I did without covering the infliction of Grandpa's multitude of 'life's lessons' on me would be akin to attempting to dissect the psychosomatic effect of attending Giuseppe Verdi's opera *Nabucco* in the actual confines of the magnificent Vienna Opera House without considering the actual music.

My father's younger brother, uncle Al, after whom I was named, went missing at the end of the war actually being one of those unfortunate souls lost on December 5, 1945 when a squadron of five Navy Avenger planes went missing in the Bermuda Triangle. So, even though the war had passed there were always ample amounts of war-related 'stuff', you know photos and magazines lying around especially in Grandma and Grandpa's house. Me, with my little pea-brain, recall finding these things more than a little unnerving in that they were constant reminders of the outrageous horrors of war, pictures showing awesome devastation and human suffering as a result of the war, especially those depicting the total destructive and debilitating force of bombing. At least, to me back then, the impact of those images was probably exactly what their originators meant to do and that was to instill absolute fear into the minds of all who saw them, fear that would last forever, especially in the burgeoning minds of the young such as me. The word 'BOMB' took on a fully-deserved, hyper-horrifying meaning to me as, even back then at the mere mention of the word, I could see the potential of my tiny five year-old 'ass' being blown to smithereens!

For whatever reason, Grandpa had disappeared in his prized '48 Ford burgundy 'woody' wagon, probably off to get a bottle of Old Grand Dad which would replace the one that Grandma found somewhere in the garage and, as was the norm, disposed of down the drain.

Anyway we found ourselves alone in the house with Grandma. Please don't get me wrong she was a very nice, very religious lady and we all loved her dearly, well as much as little brats can really 'love' anyone, you know how that goes.

Here we go into 'full disclosure' mode, somewhat reluctantly but very essential to the whole objective of this book, I really have to 'tip toe' into very, very questionable territory here. Even though I was just a few steps away from babyhood I could clearly tell that this lady, Grandma, was somewhat lacking, no very lacking in common sense and definitely not just lacking but totally void of any and all knowledge, understanding or ability to use anything mechanical...anything. A simple can opener would present an overwhelming, almost insurmountable challenge to this poor lady. This combination of lack of rudimentary mechanical skills and no common sense led to the inescapable fact that anyone around would probably find themselves victims of very questionable surprises, good or bad, at any moment when you were anywhere close to her. I am still amazed that she was allowed to do anything on her own! Grandpa's own accompanying lack of common sense only added to my consternation whenever I was around these two.

We played inside the house while Grandma was busy in the kitchen, a very scary thought on its own even when I was five or six. I can remember Grandma cooking one thing and one thing only... ham. Other than the normal potatoes, rutabagas and cabbage I can't recall ever seeing anything other than ham on her table, in fact I personally can't even remember the potatoes, rutabagas or cabbage. I am sure that she did cook other things, however, my brain only processed the ham thing. In another fit of pediatric honesty, I have to admit that I could not even believe that this lady had the mental or physical dexterity to boil ham! Again, I am rambling.

Whilst me, my brother and sisters busied ourselves in the living room entertaining ourselves with God only knows what Grandma toiled away in the kitchen. With absolutely no warning other than a very low-pitched sort of mini bang my life was about to be changed forever!
"Get out of the house " she screamed absolutely frantically at the top of her voice "it's a BOMB!!!!"

In the very instant it took me to hear that warning every damned picture that I had ever seen of burned and mutilated bodies, alive in unbelievably excruciating pain or dead after enduring excruciating pain, every last horrifying image flashed through my horror-laden brain as my brother, sisters and I ran just as fast as we could out of that house and to the supposed safety of the area behind the garage. I could be wrong but I think that we went behind the garage because that's where we saw Grandma scramble to. Anyway, there she stood sort of trembling while clutching a weird paper tube thing that was sort of like a larger, longer toilet paper roll slowly oozing some strange, gradually growing, thick whitish substance. She whispered something like "don't move, we'll be safe here until your Grandpa gets back."

She really didn't have to tell me not to move because I was petrified still envisioning a major explosion that with excruciatingly painful results would rip and shred me and my family into a bazillion pieces scattered everywhere! I waited and waited for the inevitable blast but thankfully, nothing came. Us kids all just sort of stood there looking at the mysterious whitish material oozing from Grandma's hand.

I don't know how long it was and I guess it real doesn't matter but Grandpa slowly pulled the old Ford station wagon up the driveway and stopped. He sat in the car for a moment or two just staring at us all clutched together behind the garage.

He finally got out and walked over to find out what had happened. "I think there's a bomb in the house!" was sort of what Grandma said. Grandpa managed to get some more details out of her before he slowly somewhat unenthusiastically went into the house. It was not long at all until he emerged ringing the all clear. To say that we were relieved again would be an understatement.

It turned out that once again we had fallen victim to Grandma's total lack of everything remotely relating to common sense or any sense at all. What had actually happened was that Grandma decided to try some of the then new pre-packaged, refrigerated biscuits... you know the kind in the tube that you have to smack against the edge of the countertop which pops the tube open. The damned 'bomb', as it turned out, was the sound of the biscuit tube popping open!!!

Not only did she scare the living hell out of us but we never even got the biscuits!

Over the years this has been the basis for many, many conversations. It has also raised a number of questions regarding Grandpa and Grandma and their past and why-in-the-hell anyone would think that there was a bomb in their house?

You wonder why I am absolutely surprised that I am not a total basket-case?

When it comes to Grandma and her eternal effect on the evolutionary development of my psyche, well I guess I can simply rest my case!

CHAPTER 2 – HOME SWEET HOME!

Another great example of just why I think that I should have turned out to be nothing less than a dangerous 'sub-normal' low-life, you know, a whacked-out sociopathic criminal miscreant is the following story.

When I was ready for high school for reasons still not understood by me to this very day I was enrolled in, or should I say sentenced to, a Catholic boarding school in Kingston, Ontario, which was a couple of hundred miles from our home. Regiopolis College, The Kings College, was not just a Catholic school, it was sort of a hyper-Catholic institution run by the Jesuits, the religious version of the infamous German Nazi SS, these guys were brutal!. The school itself was a huge, fully gated, limestone enclosed, limestone structure with all of the visual seduction of Alcatraz and Attica combined. The Jesuits, while running 'Regi' under the cloak of privacy, acted not in the expected role of God-fearing, people-loving priests. No, their sadistic actions were more like a group of highly skilled, above-it-all, in-your-face, Nazi concentration camp guards. Everyone conversant in Religious Orders knows that the Jesuit Order is renowned for their tough ways amongst themselves. Knowing that, it should have come as no surprise that they would impose ultra-strict rules upon those unfortunates who were in attendance at this fine institution of higher learning. To say that the Jesuits are strict is like saying that Adolph Hitler was nothing more than a pussy! The Jesuit's onerous, overly restrictive regulations disallowed almost all contact with outside influences. Included on the list of these unworthy outside influences was your own family! My sentence at Regiopolis was, and remains to this very day, a mentally unpalatable, bitter, highly questionable, offensive, very unsettling, most unpleasant experience to say the least. My feelings probably run along the same lines as those that one would feel towards Alcatraz upon being sprung from the 'Rock' after years of incarceration.

I was in no way alone in my depressed feelings towards being enrolled at the very prestigious Kings College. As a matter of fact, just in case you think that I am exaggerating the mentally oppressing effect of being placed in this institution, there were multiple unsuccessful attempts by students to bring it all to an end and unfortunately, during my tenure at this institution, one successful suicide. Everything about being at Regi was depressing, and the considerable distance from home only added to the constant and overwhelming lost feelings, in that I knew it was all but impossible for me to get home. The rule whereby we were allowed only three or four visits home each year did very little to alleviate these feelings of devastating isolation. The main consequence of these restrictions on getting home was that our visits home took on a far, far more prominent role in our lives.

Now, let's get back to the subject of weird things happening in my life. I recall one specific holiday. Thanksgiving was one of those special occasions when we were allowed to go home, albeit just for a long weekend. Believe me there are no words strong enough to convey my excitement and euphoria surrounding these infrequent trips home. To accommodate the travel time, the priests were nice enough to let us out of school early on Fridays in order for us to catch the trains that would carry us home. In my case, there was a train from Toronto that passed through Kingston at around 5 PM. This would get me to the station into St. Anne de Bellevue at around 10 o'clock. The train station was on the outskirts of the village, about five or six miles from our house. The normal routine was for Mom to drive to the station and pick me up, however, sometimes it was someone else who would show up, with our family, you never really knew what was going to materialize until you saw the whites, and most of the time, red blood-shot whites of their eyes.

This particular weekend had not started very well in that as of Friday morning I had still not received any travel money, nor my train tickets, from either Mom or Dad. The money was always sort of routinely late, so I did not get overly concerned. I had tried on numerous occasions to telephone them, but for some reason, just could not get through. I ended up borrowing what I could from my friends and luckily, it was just enough to buy my round-trip ticket. In any case, the five o'clock train came, I got on, and was on my way home.

It was Fall, so it was getting dark early and the weather was getting cold and true to form, it was cold by the time I got off of the train. I was the only one who got off at the St. Annes station, which was not that uncommon, and the place had already been closed down for the night. My family had not yet arrived, so I watched the train leave and slowly disappear in the distance.

I sat down on one of the benches and waited for a while. I would have tried to phone but I had only been able to borrow just what the ticket had cost, so I was flat broke. I sat there for an hour or so. I was getting pretty cold, so I decided that I would start to walk. There were only two ways to get to the station from our house, so I knew the chances of intercepting my family on their way to get me were good. I had my suitcase, which was not that heavy, but it surely was a pain to carry. I dared not leave it anywhere, so I just kept walking. It was dark and cold, after all it was getting pretty late. I was speculating on why nobody had shown up to get me. I figured that the Chevy station wagon must have been the culprit. It would break down at the worst of times. The car probably just would not start! I also considered that maybe they had taken the other road and they would loop around and find me.

It was close to midnight as I made my way past the veteran's hospital. Oh yes, the veteran's hospital. This place could easily qualify on its own as another weird thing that intruded into my brain in my younger, and very formative, life. Even though I was in my teens, I still got the 'willies' when I had to walk by that place. Getting older and more understanding only intensified the uneasy feelings and spine-tingling fright because you were able to fully comprehend the danger posed by the hundreds of criminally insane occupants at this hospital, I walked a little faster. I was less than a mile from the house now, so I had it 'made in the shade' as we used to say at school. The suitcase now felt like a ton of bricks. No matter which arm I chose, or how I attempted to carry that damned thing, it was now becoming painful. Five miles is quite a trek at the end of a long day. When it's cold, you're hungry and thirsty, and you have a stupid suitcase to carry, it soon becomes a marathon, luckily, I was almost there.

The chilly weather was getting to me and I just kept getting colder and colder as I approached the end of the driveway to our house. It was a few minutes past midnight when I finally made it to the stone wall that surrounded our yard. I quickly turned into the driveway. Our house lay back quite a ways from the road, about two thirds of the way to the lake. I stopped at the end of the driveway, put my suitcase down, and just stood there for a moment, I was finally home.

It was very quiet, too quiet in fact, there wasn't a sound. It was cold enough that I could see my breath swirling around my face. I could also see the house but it was strangely quiet. Not only was it quiet, but there were no lights on in the house, there were no lights on the porch, there were no lights on the garage, not one. I thought that to be rather strange. Even more puzzling was the fact that there were no cars anywhere to be seen in the driveway. The garage was right at the entrance to the driveway so I slowly walked over and looked through the windows into the garage. There were no cars in the garage in fact, there was nothing in the garage at all! No tools, no garbage cans, no trunks, rakes or hoes, nothing!

Now I was really puzzled. I walked back over to my suitcase and again, just stared at the house. The moon kept peeking through the clouds and you could see its sparkling reflections atop the waves on the lake. It was a pretty sight indeed. As I watched the sparkling lake, I came to realize that I could see the reflections directly through the windows of the house! There were no curtains, no drapes, no blinds, and all of the downstairs doors were wide open.

After a few moments of mental assessment, I mustered up enough courage to actually approach the house. Not having a clue as to what was going on, I did so with some caution. The old floorboards creaked and groaned as I climbed the steps up to the verandah and walked across to the large front window. That was the only real noise that I heard, there was definitely no noise coming from anywhere in the house. I stuck my face right up to the front picture windows and stared into the house. I could not believe my eyes, the damned house was empty! Not a stick of furniture or any other item of furnishing to be seen. All of the pictures were gone, the baby-grand piano was gone, the place was empty!

I tried opening the front door, but it was locked. I walked around to the back door, and it too was locked, not that it would have done me any good, there was nobody there. Besides, they had taken everything with them. They were gone, my whole family was gone!

My choices of what to do next were few to say the least. Although I was in a state of severe distress and shock, I still had some mental processing ability left. I knew that my sister Jackie, after recently getting married, was living in the village of Ste. Annes so off I went walking back to the village. I do not remember any details of my walk back or how and when I showed up at Jackie's doorstep, but I did. I'm sure that we must have talked for a while. She did tell me that the family had in fact moved, to a town called Beaconsfield, some ten miles or so from Ste. Annes. She also informed me that it would be a further waste of my time to try to telephone my family because they had gone away for the holidays! She was right, they had gone off to who knew where without me!

In any case, she kindly made a bed up for me, and I, confused, confounded and amazed, went to sleep. I awoke in the morning still somewhat dismayed at this rather strange, turn of events. Jackie and her husband Arthur and I had a nice visit the next day, actually laughing and having a good time.

We did have a nice visit. We enjoyed a great turkey dinner and then Jackie kindly made turkey sandwiches for me. After a short rest, they took me to the train station where I boarded the train and again I was off and on my way back to school!

As if this whole episode was not bad enough already, it was a good thing that I had those sandwiches for, when I got back to school a day early, there was nothing open other than the infirmary. I had to book into 'sick bay', with only my sandwiches and fond memories of my visit with my mostly missing family to tide me over for the next day! Whatever possessed Mom and Dad to move the family without telling me? I'll never know.

This story doesn't finish here for, as if this weren't enough to supply an ample amount of mental fodder for my entire life, on my very next visit home, they were again gone! Mom and Dad had taken the rest of the family on vacation without telling me! At least this time they had not moved. I remember just giving in and staying overnight at a friend's house. I got on a train the very next morning and went back to school. I really had no choice! Strange, you bet!

I am not overly weird or crazy as a result of these rather strange goings on in my younger life. Nor do I dwell on these things for great lengths of time doing the 'why me?' thing. I haven't become a sociopathic, crazed, cross-addicted, diabolical mass-murderer, hell, I'm not even anti-social!

What the hell is wrong? WHY NOT ME? What really puzzles me is not that I never ever got any answers from Mom or Dad as to how these events happened. What also puzzles me is why I took these occurrences as being somewhat normal! I never pressed for an answer, I didn't even ask more than a couple of times! It probably didn't matter anyway because I'm sure the answer would have been a really weird, strange, and silly one anyway. I can't, for the life of me, think of any answer that wouldn't be! But, I just never got one. It's strange because Mom and Dad were not mean, cruel, stupid, or foolish people, they just acted a tad irresponsible at times.

It would have been really neat to have some deep, wild, thought provoking, philosophical answer to how these occurrences happened, you know the kind that only makes sense after years and years of mental digestion and regurgitation. Maybe they actually had an answer like that and I never pressed them enough for it! Maybe there was some mysterious reason for their strange behavior.

No way, the answer is simply that they were from Cincinnati, and that's the way people from Cincinnati used to do things!

CHAPTER 3 - THE FAMILY TREE
(actually a family bramble bush)

In my humble opinion our 'family tree' is really much more akin to a bramble bush, a thicket, a thorny undergrowth that hides whatever lurks beneath and will do little else but inflict pain with each and every attempt to retrieve anything from it. Even worse is once you are in its grasp even more pain and mental suffering will result of any and all efforts to get out and away from its bloodletting clutches. I know this sounds like maybe a 'bit' of overkill for sure but I can assure you that there are many relatives as well as strangers that have the mental scars and wounds to back me up.

Remember that I was in my very young and formative, psyche building years when I first started to hear and mentally 'take in' stories or, I should probably say rumors, of many of my relatives' rather checkered pasts. As I grew older and wiser these stories have continued to be bandied around and retold in many different forms from all sources imaginable, inside the family as well as independents. A substantial number these stories have also been gathering detail, albeit foggy detail, as they keep rolling down memory lane. The basic stories, however, keep being regurgitated year after year after year much to the chagrin of many family members but also much to the inquisitive delight of other tribal members such as me who look back in awe at the weird and wacky twists and turns of our family background.

Two stories about Grandpa Mueller immediately come to mind. The first was actually told to me by my father one late night out on the porch at the Lodge. It was about Grandpa's involvement in running liquor for the 'Mob', yes you guessed it as in Scarface, Al Capone's gang. I never really heard a lot more about this part of Grandpa's past, however, it would not surprise me. I certainly had much more than ample validation of the second story which in a somewhat convoluted way only adds credence to the first one.

Firstly, during the period of time when there was Federally mandated prohibition Grandpa was working for the Shack Truck Company, a company that specialized in those massive and rather ornate fire trucks that were very common in the 1930s and 1940s.

Looking Back on a Warped but Wonderful Childhood

I was told that he was one of the 'pin-stripers' who used to hand-paint those fine contrasting lines, normally in gold, around the fenders and cowls of the trucks. He also used to paint those elaborate emblems on the doors that would distinguish and personalize each truck. Now that is what I was told, however, I have great reservations as to the veracity of these claims. Grandpa, God bless his well-pickled soul, was a drinker and a pretty heavy one at that. The combination of hangovers and hyper-quality, accurate pin-striping from the hands of a heavy drinker just doesn't cut it but, that again is just my opinion.

Let's assume that Dad was in fact telling it 'like it was' and that Gramp's was in fact able to fulfill the steady requirements for pin-striping these trucks with near-surgical accuracy. The City of Chicago was one of Shack Truck's most important clients and as a result would be given very special treatment. It was time to replace one of the aging fire trucks in Chicago and somehow Grandpa was chosen as the guy to travel to the city and physically secure not only the order but all of the designs for the artwork for the pin-striping, emblems and insignias. Within a few days he returned with the order and artwork in tow with one caveat, he was to personally deliver the new fire truck to Chicago and bring the old one back to Cincinnati. A rather odd request indeed but one that would be accommodated by Shack.

A few months went by and Grandpa was in the new truck on his way to Chicago and after a few more days he was triumphantly returning to Cincinnati with the old, well-used and I suspect heavier than suspected fire truck.

The second story has been validated many times over by far too numerous sources to be anything less than true, probably embellished and exaggerated repeatedly over time but authentic none-the-less.

The story goes that when working for the Shack Truck Co. Grandpa had disappeared, poof he was gone, vanished into thin air without a trace! Grandma, of course, was a mess and totally devastated, in fact the whole family was at a total loss for any explanation as to what had happened to the man and why?

As is sometimes the case in solving mysteries a serendipitous situation or clue emerges out of nowhere. Coincidental happenings also can add valuable information which may assist in finding a solution.

Such was the case when it came to finding Grandpa. Wouldn't you know it, one of the young, obviously less-than-innocent secretaries had also gone missing at the exact same time as did Grandpa! To make a long story short and to avoid the nasty, sexually-laced descriptives of the event that at the time I heard it had my little innocent ears in a buzz I will tell you that they found Grandpa. They also found the errant Shack Company 'poopsie' shacked-up (pun intended!) and trying to put out their own 'personal fires' in a quaint and cozy lakeside cabin in the Mountain View area of the Adirondack Mountains in the real upstate New York. Making the story even better was that this particular love nest was actually part of a group of Scarface's Mob's official 'getaway' mountain retreats.

In retrospect, if this story is true, and I have few reasons to doubt that it is, then it would appear that this probably was nothing more, or nothing less, than payment for running the fire truck and its possible sudsy alcoholic contents from Chicago to Cincinnati. This incident, I believe, could have been one of the contributing factors in Grandma having very, very tight reins on innocent, lay-back old George, otherwise known to us as Gramps.

Throughout most of my life I have been accused of being a careless daredevil, operating with a clear disregard for personal safety coupled with a serious lack of respect for danger. I will be the first to admit that these accusations are for the most part true. I, as did most of my immediate family, seemed to seek out the more exhilarating and stimulating things in life. A prime example of this wild-side personality trait is the roller coaster. Our whole family simply loves to ride them, we cannot get enough of them. Moreover, the faster, wilder, and more frightening the ride, the better we like them. It's that ungoverned brain-twisting, gut-wrenching, stomach-churning, dizzying feeling that does it. Some people have no desire to experience this type of excitement, and that certainly is their rightful option. I might not agree with them but I do personally understand them. I often wonder what really makes the difference, however,

Looking Back on a Warped but Wonderful Childhood

I think I know the base root for this type of thrill seeking personality. I bring this up in this discussion on my family because the seeds for my personal love of heart-stopping fear and crazy, out-of-control, spin me around till I'm silly type of fast and furious action were very well-sown, watered, harvested, and served up on a regular basis by many loving members of my family. This trait, however, was forged into my psyche, and subsequently honed and polished to amazing perfection by three main influences, Uncle Gerry, Uncle Bud, and Dad! My unbridled love of speed is traceable directly to my Dad. My intrigue and infatuation with danger and fright, I suspect, can be tracked directly to my Uncles Gerry and my Mother's brother, Norbert, Uncle Bud to us kids.

My Dad was a car racer at heart but unfortunately for the other motorists on the roads that he traveled, as well as assorted local police departments, he never had the time or opportunity to race professionally. Instead he practiced his real chosen profession by racing on the public roads, everywhere, and anytime he went anywhere. He simply loved going fast. He would speed to get quickly to a place where he could really speed! This was back in the days when two-lane highways were the order of the day, and passing lines of slow moving cars (to Dad, anything traveling less than the speed of sound) was a heart-stopping and truly death-defying feat, definitely not to be attempted by mere mortal motoring milque-toasts. To get the most out of his innate need for speed, Dad always had cars that were truly capable of shattering actual speed records so we were accustomed to going dangerously fast at a very early age. My youngest sister was actually brought home from her place of birth, some 25 miles at a rapid rate of speed I am sure in a Jaguar XK120 with the top down! As I said, we were programmed for speed from the very beginning of our precious and strange little lives.

Then there was Uncle Gerry. Uncle Gerry was supposed to be a really good guy. I have heard few bad remarks, if any, about Uncle Gerry. I do not remember a lot about Uncle Gerry but I do remember waiting anxiously with my siblings for his visits. The fact that he was from Dad's side of the family most likely played a major role in this guy's ability to appear perfectly normal most of the time then, with little or no warning, become possessed by some overwhelming, mentally debilitating power turning him into a maniacal idiot.

Even though I was very young, I think I had this transformation pegged. As far as I could determine, this metamorphosis took place only when Uncle Gerry got behind the wheel of his most prized possession, an old 1939 Ford sedan. The fact that it was a Ford, as opposed to a Studebaker or Chrysler I think was of no consequence and not the reason for my recall of this automobile. The cause for this car sticking out and leaving an indelible mark on my brain was that this was a car in which most of the rear floor was missing, rusted out, as in gone! Now, when you are a child of four or five years old, and placed unrestrained in the back of a car, the floor becomes a very important platform for you to be able to safely move around. To be placed on the back seat of a car without a floor was like being put on the very edge of a cliff with ragged rocks and ripping edges, with the cliff moving at a relatively high rate of speed. When you add in the elements of having no sane adult supervision in the rear, being totally unrestrained on that back seat, the car going at excessive speeds, slam-dunk multiple stops and intentional, very erratic driving to the mix, you have all the essential ingredients to scramble any little kids brain for life!

The object of this outrageous game was for us kids to hang our heads over the side of the seat and watch the street go by below! We used to hang on to whatever we could, grabbing on for dear life, hoping and praying that we would not be flung off the seat and down through the gaping 'black hole of certain death' in the floor, never to be seen again! What a great game for little kids! What, you don't agree? I hate to say it but it must not have been quite as bad as I have stated here, for us kids could not get enough of Uncle Gerry's wild ride. It was like having our own combination of Disney, Coney Island, and Freddy Krueger. Not only that, it was free. Now I have to pay to even attempt to feel 'stuff' like that!

Good or bad, Uncle Gerry was not around all that often. To compensate for the increased safety to us kids from his absence, God made sure that we would not let down our guard and fall into a false sense of security or feel safe and non-threatened. God gave us Uncle Bud!

Uncle Bud was my mother's brother. As is somewhat typical in my family, he went through a rather strange metamorphosis in his working life which, I suspect, dramatically affected his personal life as well. Uncle Bud started his working life as a steam locomotive mechanic, a regular dirty blue-collar guy. Unfortunately, or, fortunately if you consider the ultimate outcome, he suffered a very serious, mechanic-work terminating injury. I have no idea what length of time, extent of rehab, or anything else that contributed to the awesome fateful transmutation. I am quite sure that it must have been extensive. To the delight of some, and to the chagrin of many others, after his recovery Uncle Bud emerged as a full-fledged, blood draining, psychologically painful, perfectly groomed and postured mortician! This proves beyond any reasonable doubt that God truly does have a sense of humor and it is a pretty weird and wild one at that. Virtually everything that Uncle Bud needed to fulfill his real desires as well as to fully utilize his real talents lay behind the doors of the funeral parlor.

To me back then, and honestly to this day, Uncle Bud seemed to have only two real goals in life, firstly to scare all of us kids to death or secondly, to physically burn our little butts to a crisp.

I would be remiss if I did not venture into a very questionable, somewhat distasteful area at this point so let's get this one out of the way, post-haste. Never mind speed or crazy-ass driving with us aboard but, or should I say *butt*, another of one of my relatives weird obsessions that left an indelible mark on my little developing psyche. Whenever us kids were around Uncle Bud and his wife Aunt Carol for that matter we were in constant fear of the dreaded 'physic' thing, 'physic' being the Cincinnati name for enema! Come on now, you've gone this far so just keep reading.

The mere mention of any physical or emotional complaint in front of these two would trigger the desire to sort of tag-team us in this 'physic' thing. Any mention of discomfort would always culminate in one of us kids being grabbed, subjected to a series of humiliating and rather uncomfortable events with the 'crescendo' being one member of their tag-team holding you prisoner in the bath tub while the other probed, poked and plunged till we all had had enough. They of course would always win. Without question this activity would be more than frowned upon today, most likely being deemed highly illegal, even in today's rather liberal society.

Who knows, this was in Cincinnati and maybe everyone did this back then! They were so intent on this enema thing, that even loose, (sorry again, no pun intended) statements made by another kid would have you in their weird, soapy grasp. Again, we all survived, so my representation of these traumatic experiences may be an over-exaggeration. It doesn't really matter, to me it was still very, very weird! Unlike the life-threatening, heart stopping experiences in Uncle Gerry's old Ford, we did not clamor and beg for more of this action!

There was one other thing that we all knew. When you were around Uncle Bud you *were* going to get the living crap scared out of you! He had a host of things that he loved to use as disguises and he was absolutely the best at manipulating people into the most advantageous spot for him to get them. Worse yet was that he lived on the upper floor of a funeral parlor! When you went to see him, you knew that you were only a step away from death, probably your own, and most likely from a heart attack!

Another quick story to illustrate the above. As stated, Uncle Bud lived above the funeral parlor. There were three ways to get up to the apartment. One was an enclosed stairway on the outside of the building, another was through the parlor itself and yet another was through the basement which was a pathway that would take you directly by the dreaded embalming rooms.

Many of our family members were in Cincinnati probably for a funeral. In any case one evening we had all congregated outside in the back yard of Uncle Buds place, the 'spooky' funeral parlor. At some point in time one of my sisters had to use the washroom and left to go upstairs to the apartment. Little did we know that Uncle Bud, knowing full well that someone sooner or later would have to get upstairs, had locked the doors to both the funeral parlor as well as the outside stairway. He did so with the premeditation and forethought of any murderer knowing that his actions would force whoever wanted to get upstairs through the basement.

In short order my sister reappeared after attempting the other two entrances. Now she had always been hesitant to even go to the funeral parlor and was hyper-reluctant to go anywhere near the basement where the horror-filled embalming rooms were. Uncle Bud just sat there knowing full well that nature would soon take over and force her to take the dark pathway to the apartment. He was right and she slowly but surely disappeared into the basement.

The other gathered family members just kept talking and laughing, totally oblivious to the fact that Uncle Bud had also vanished somewhat stealthily.

Moments later were we all startled by a truly blood-curdling scream emanating from the basement. We all rushed to the doorway to find my sister in a state of dazed, semi-consciousness, another victim of Uncle Bud's rather morbid sense of humor. He had slid off to one of the embalming rooms where he covered himself in a white sheet and waited 'in ambush' for my poor sister, jumping out of the embalming room right in front of her as she cautiously made her way along the darkened hallway. I cannot really remember whether or not she required medical attention, however, I believe she did.

Perhaps his greatest talent came out only when, like Uncle Gerry, he became crazed by his most prized possession, his super-dooper, trusty, stainless steel Zippo lighter! He would take out this damned thing, set it ablaze, and run after us kids with it, trying for his life to set us ablaze! This was no regular Zippo either, this thing was an industrial strength baby that had fire and flames a foot long spewing from its triple-plated, stainless steel-hinged head. As lighters go, it must have been awesome! We would start running for dear life at the very clicking sound of the spring-loaded head being flipped open. Uncle Bud, I'm convinced, was not kidding either. If he had caught any of us kids, he would have in fact lit our little butts, and probably laughed as we popped, fizzed, and bubbled into the next dimension. What added to my mental anguish was that I knew that our great Grandmother, on his side of the family, had burned to death in what was supposed to have been an unfortunate kitchen accident. I certainly have my doubts. It was probably at the hands of Uncle Bud testing his new Zippo! I also wonder why he didn't try to douse the fire with one of the ever-present soapy, water-filled enema bags!

My Grandma Mueller was a very religious person to put it lightly. There were stories bandied about regarding her claims to have actually seen the Blessed Virgin Mary standing at the foot of her bed. Whatever the truth, two of her daughters, my aunts, became nuns ultimately residing at a local convent which was also an orphanage, which is central in yet another story in this book.

This part of the story also gets a little weird in that one of my aunts, after years and years of 'being married to God' decided to leave the convent and experience life on the outside, including a full-fledged relationship with a man and having to actually pay bills! It did not take long for her to realize that life on the outside is quite challenging, so she pulled up her personal stakes and took her now less-than-sacred backside back to the orphanage where she was actually forgiven for her 'earthly sins' and allowed to go back to her prior 'sister' status! One can only imagine the off-color conversations that must have taken place in the holy confines of the orphanage after that.

Grandma's religious fervor, coupled with her daughters becoming sisters of the Catholic Church, allowed for unprecedented access to the officers of the Church, those who were responsible for the many business decisions that were made at the local and regional level.

Now let me introduce Uncle Leo, one of Grandma's brothers, who was in the metal finishing business. Through a series of circumstances, 'creative marketing' and divine intervention (God, I hope not!) Uncle Leo found himself in a position to offer the Church a philanthropic deal that they could not refuse. He would refinish all of the gold, precious gem-studded chalices and assorted priceless articles of all the churches in the diocese... at no charge.

A very, very generous offer indeed and one that the Church could not, and indeed did not, refuse.

Uncle Leo traveled the far-reaching highways and byways of the diocese philanthropically collecting these precious treasures of the Church. He would do his 'magic' with the Church's tarnished 'booty' after which he would again travel the diocese returning the glittering holy masterpieces to their rightful hallowed stewards.

'Magic' has numerous meanings and manifestations and Uncle

Leo's magic was really a consecrated disappearing/reappearing act in which he would make the solid gold articles and their prized gems disappear replacing the lot with simple inexpensive gold-plated white metal look-alikes studded with cheap costume jewelry stones. He would 'fence' the real stuff and, of course, pocket the proceeds.

The Church somehow discovered Uncle Leo's 'magic' but decided that it was best, and far less embarrassing, to simply 'sweep it under the blessed rug' as if nothing happened. Just in case you are wondering, Uncle Leo died of old age, not a lightning bolt from the Heavens!

These were just some of our relatives! There were also an abundance of strange, weird types coming and going. Many of these were not only weird and strange, but displayed an assortment of characteristics reserved in the depths of the psychiatric manuals to describe only the criminally insane amongst us.

A great example of this was a character introduced to me as Dr. Fred Bland. The good doctor was all of four and a half feet tall in his Jackboots, standing on a gravestone. He drove an English Allard J2R sports car that was black on the outside, black on the inside, black canvas top, with black-walled tires and oh yes, wire wheels that were also painted black. Lucifer's chosen ride if there ever was one! He also sported a monocle and spoke with a very high-pitched, very broken, German accent. Fortunately for me, I only saw him a few times, however, when I did he was wearing a full-length trench coat that was black, and black trousers that were tucked into the black Jackboots!

He was very weird indeed and what was worse, was that he wore gloves that covered a prosthetic metal right hand, a hand by the way that he once threatened to pull a quivering portal part of my lower anatomy out through my nasal passages! This was really not a nice guy at all and one that I suspect should not have been allowed anywhere close to children, actually anywhere close to anything!

CHAPTER 4 – THE HAMILTON YEARS

As stated in the prologue, this whole story actually has its own birth with a small miracle in a small hospital in the small hamlet of Hamilton, Ohio, in the hospital in which I was born. Hamilton is a 'bed room' suburb of Cincinnati, Ohio and one of those places that you either love or can do without, count me amongst the latter.

I have asserted for years and years now that one of, if not the main reason that I am actually a happy, gregarious individual is not only that I was born in Cincinnati but, more importantly, that I through great luck and sheer happenstance got out of there early, in my case at the age of 5.

Believe me it was definitely not all 'warm and fuzzy' in my life after my extraction from the Cincinnati area, however, I honestly believe that it was far better than what it would have been if we had not moved from Hamilton.

When we were in Hamilton we lived in a pretty nice middle class house. What I remember most about the house was that there was a semi-circular walkway off of the short driveway. From birth I could not get enough wheeled vehicles. I had the normal kid's tricycle, a great American Flyer wood-sided wagon and my real favorite, a fire-engine red pedal-powered fire truck and I wore the wheels off of all of them. That walkway and connected driveway formed my own imaginary Indianapolis Motor Speedway and I would hold my own personal 500 mile races whenever I could on that track.

The real Indy 500 was a regular subject in our house. Dad was actually a mechanical engineer who was also an official consultant mechanic to the Miller Racing Team when they would compete at Indy. We would attend the races as kids, most of our time being spent under the bleachers collecting hundreds of discarded cardboard beer cups seeing which one of us kids could stack these cups the highest without them falling over.

Dad was also a 'closet' race car driver who unfortunately never got the opportunity to officially demonstrate his racing skills in a sanctioned event instead, even more unfortunately, destroying a couple of his personal automobiles on empty race tracks much to the chagrin and horror of Mom and others who watched. My need for speed was a genetic side-effect of being my Dad's son.

Early memories are indeed an integral part of the foundation upon which ones psyche develops and if that is the case then these Hamilton years make up the very cornerstone upon which the actual foundation arose. There may be a fault in my 'foundation' for I admit that although most of these remembrances are ones that I can close my eyes and still see them as clearly as the day they happened, however, some of my so-called special memories may or may not be mine at all! I know that doesn't make much sense but from the first days of my little brain being able to absorb and retain the spoken word I have heard numerous strange and weird tales from the mouths of my older and much wiser siblings. My brain somehow adopted them and placed them in with the memoirs that I know are legitimate.

Stories like the one of Dad actually dive-bombing the house in some oil-spewing old *Sopwith Camel* bi-plane as Mom hung clothes out to dry in the back yard. Oh yes, I have to add that these clothes were occasionally blood-stained, the blood coming from the basement floor and walls, allegedly from killing chickens down there. Why they would not have done the normal outdoors slaughter thing could be the basis for a whole other story.

I am sure that my sisters may be horrified at these 'special' recollections and they may have a totally different take on these 'special' memories as to when and where they happened, maybe even if they ever happened at all, however, in my brain they definitely are there. Besides, this is my book and until someone writes another version of them, this is what I am going with.

On my defense I cannot imagine how I could remember details such as being in the Buick convertible in the 'lab' episode and the fact that the *Sopwith Camel* plane had a simple longitudinal bench seat with no belts; how else would I know this, whether I was there or not, someone had to feed me these details of these truly special memoirs!

One of these 'special' memories that is embedded in my mind is what could be called Mom's 'Walk of Despair'. This is a prime example of the above because I've heard about it so much that it has taken on a spot in the part of my brain reserved for only those actual events and situations that I genuinely experienced.

Most likely not surprising to those close to our family but none-the-less unfortunate for Mom she must have found herself in an extremely questionable and mental-challenging situation. I would assume that it revolved around Dad and her marriage to this man. Dealing with Dad had to be a huge challenge, especially as a wife. He was set in his ways, after all his father, my grandfather, was an open door 'closet' Nazi sympathizer candidly receiving Nazi-championing newspapers from Da Faderland itself on a weekly basis. Retrospectively, there was a huge Germanic population in the Cincinnati area so support for the Nazis back then was probably not all that rare or scorned upon.

Anyway, I am quite certain that Mom had perfectly valid reasons for her sometimes erratic behavior. When confronted by whatever personal situations that were challenging she would elevate it to the status of an immediate absolute dilemma. Mom many times would react or I propose, possibly with very specific goal-oriented premeditation, act in a very public and very 'theatrical' exhibition for our neighbors' quasi-educational entertainment.

Such was the case when it came to Mom's very public 'Walks of Desperation'. When triggered by some unsavory situation in her (our?) life she would simply go and pack her suitcase and then proceed down the street in a very unceremonious parade for all to see. She would be followed, of course, by us kids crying, screaming and begging her to come back home, wow that will also bend your little brain when you are four or five!

I am the first to admit that Dad was different to say the least and he absolutely had to be more than a handful in any effort to control him. Marriage, if nothing else, probably gives a struggling spouse at least the mental perception of having some right to at least attempt to place some reasonable control over an errant partner. Dad also constantly had a gaggle of loud, boisterous, drunken social misfits that always seemed to be 'looming' around the house. Weird and highly questionable idiosyncrasies aside, most of the time he actually seemed to be a relatively normal human being gainfully employed as a draftsman at Lima Hamilton Corporation, a diverse conglomerate that produced many products including steam locomotives. The corporate headquarters in which Dad worked was located in Hamilton.

Another of my first 'special' memories, special meaning any remembrances that disallowed me to ever forget them, normally resulting from their shock or absolute fright value, involved the 'Lab' at Lima Hamilton.

Maybe Dad was a workaholic or just maybe there were more sinister reasons involved but Dad routinely worked at night. Occasionally, he would load us kids into the car and take us with him. He would stop at the neighborhood donut shop, buy a bag of goodies which we could later ingest as we patiently waited in the car of course. The 'Lab' sat beside some railroad tracks which should not be a surprise to anyone, after all they did make trains.

It's not the donuts, the Lab or us kids sitting alone in a car that made it so unforgettable, it was the ride from the donut shop to the Lab that used to scare the living hell out of my young, budding brain. It would normally be dark out and Dad would take what he called a shortcut to the lab. The shortcut was actually the single train track that ran behind the donut shop and past the Lab. He would slowly pull the car onto the tracks and gradually we would make our rather bumpy ride to the lab where he would pull off the tracks and park. What made this ride so frightening was that he would constantly tell us to keep an eye out for oncoming trains! I used to freak my little butt off. In reality he knew that the only train traffic on those particular tracks were locomotives being shipped to or from the factory, we never were in any danger, at least not from trains.

I've covered the planes, trains and automobiles but I would be somewhat remiss if I didn't cover the submarines.

During the War the Lima Hamilton Corporation shifted its focus to a Naval military mission to assist in the design and engineering for submarines and Dad was amongst those selected employees given government security clearance for this honorable endeavor. With the War over and dwindling in its rear-view mirrors Lima Hamilton went back to its focus on the manufacturing of locomotives. They may have put their involvement in submarines out of their corporate minds, however, the American Federal Government had other ideas launching an official espionage investigation involving one of Dad's German co-workers with a name that I could never pronounce let alone spell. The stories surrounding this went on for years and we, us kids, were told that in the ensuing legal process Dad was either called, or volunteered, to act as a simple character witness for this guy. Dad was normally a very convincing guy but not always. The guy was immediately found guilty and sentenced, probably to death. The questions that still linger in my mind is why Dad would have been involved in this deal at all. The fact that Dad was allowed to roam free at least gives me some mental comfort.

The Hamilton years were truly developmental, with the emphasis on *mental*. I remember one evening as I did my final laps for the day around my imaginary race track I saw my Brother George sitting on the stoop, crying and weeping in an almost unbelievable display of despair. I quickly got out of my pedal car, actually a fire truck, and went to see what was wrong.
"What's the matter?" I asked.
"Al Jolson is dead" was his sobbing, sniffling snot-filled response! Wow, I was at a loss for even immature words let alone anything that could come close to comforting for an older brother. Al Jolson had passed and George, at the tender age of eight obviously at that moment seemingly could find no valid reason to continue on in life. Gosh!

Why that stuck with me to this very day I have not a clue. There actually may have been a deep, dark hidden psychological reason though, Grandpa Panko, my Mom's father. Grandpa Panko you see on the occasional weekend would blacken his face as to look like a black person, an ugly black person at that, dress up in a dress and a wig so that he resembled a black *woman*, oh yes, an very ugly black woman and head out for whatever, wherever. At least that's my version based upon the mental recall of what I would have seen through my little non racial eyes at the age of 4 or 5.

There was, however, a much less questionable, more palatable reason for my remembrance. What I saw as very strange behavior was in reality not so strange at all. Grandpa was actually part of an amateur 'minstrel' group that would escape from reality by heading out to freely roam the dingy streets of the Cincinnati area looking for who-in-the-hell really knows what. Now having just wrote what I wrote, this explanation doesn't really ring in as anything less than weird after all.

As I have stated many, many times Cincinnati does something awesome to your brain, even young, innocent ones and is one great place... to be from!

CHAPTER 5 – SENTENCED TO RAWDON, QUEBEC!

This story begins when I was just a young lad of four years, going on five. Dad was a draftsman at Lima Hamilton Corporation, a conglomerate that manufactured amongst other things, mid-sized steam locomotives. I guess that we were simply the typical middle-class family living in a suburb of Cincinnati, Ohio.

Through some strange twist of fate Dad had accepted a challenging position as the Vice President of the Canadian Locomotive Company, a Canadian subsidiary of Lima Hamilton that produced even bigger steam locomotives. The acceptance of this new position brought about a myriad of hyper-dramatic changes not only for Dad but for the entire family, two of which were absolutely pivotal.

This was truly a 'good news, bad news' deal. Firstly, the 'good' news was that Dad's income was increased a couple of hundred percent in a very, very short period of time. The bad news was that the entire family, plus one questionable addition, was moved to the 'Great White North', Hockeyland Central, the Montreal, Quebec area of Canada.

We first settled into a little hamlet in the province named Rawdon, a 'cutesy' little village in a very, very rural setting some sixty or seventy miles from Montreal. I'm not positive, but I believe that the name Rawdon probably came from one of the native Indian tribes and actually meant 'land of absolutely no value'! In any case, this sleepy little village of Rawdon and its inhabitants were the lucky unsuspecting recipients of our tribe. Our tribe was a strange one indeed consisting of Mom, Dad, six children, and in true theatrical fashion, a non-related girl of seventeen or so named Dorothy. Now, you have to admit that just this introduction of Dorothy into this tale makes you want to continue to read this story. Throughout my life, even after many, many questions to Mom and Dad in a genuine search for the truth, I never received a really good answer as to why this girl was brought along. I could be wrong, and I hope that I am, however, I strongly suspect that the truth would easily qualify as material for adult audiences only, thank you very much. Even with a mature audience, I suspect that only the most liberal would enjoy the deep, dark secrets of that questionable part of this story, our own Dorothy and probably a much more out of the ordinary version of a 'yellow brick road'!

In addition to the main gaggle of characters in this account, there was always an assortment of very different 'clingons' that would drift in and out of our 'space', seemingly at their whim. When I suggest some sort of 'drop in' this was one really 'in the sticks' place with no TV, few telephones, intermittent electricity, hell, even automobiles were rare and a very recent addition to this most rustic of rustic communities.

The house in which we found ourselves had only a wood stove, you know the kind that looked and operated like a smaller version of a steam locomotive's boiler actually utilizing wood instead of coal for fuel, but requiring the same amount of filth gathering toil and dexterity to operate. People now think these things are cute and maybe wood stoves are cute in the movies, but this was no movie, this was our daily life! Again I rely upon my overworked little brain as I was only five or six years old so I may be wrong but I'm not even sure that there was a furnace in the house. Aside from the lack of modern amenities, the house really was pretty neat. It was a converted bed and breakfast, or small hotel, and was a rather pleasant place with many strange but highly unique characteristics aside from the aforementioned lack of modern-day standards.

The house rested on a beautiful little lake with very slippery banks, take it from me, they were very, very slippery! The first thing I did when we arrived was run towards the lake to inspect its mysterious depths. Just about the exact moment I heard Mom hollering to "stay away from the lake", you guessed it! As I said, them banks was really slippery.

Was it the perfect setting? If you like mosquitoes, black flies, Canadian geese, moose, deer, ice, and cold, snowy weather it was magnificent. Most of us kids were lucky in that we were too young to even recognize misery, so we really had no idea that our little butts were solidly in its ever tightening grasp!

I don't recall a great deal about our family's stay in Rawdon, but I do have a few fond, and a few strange, memories.

I recall waking up one morning and wandering outside onto the porch. I was awestruck, my little pea brain went into overdrive. To my absolute amazement when I gazed out onto what just the day before used to be the lake, was now just a rather deep, very muddy, swamp-like crater. Sort of like the Moon's Tranquility Base, right after a monsoon-like downpour. For reasons probably best unknown to all the law-abiding Rawdon constituents, they had actually drained the water out of the lake leaving a huge mess cluttered with an assortment of rusty objects and other mysterious items in full public view, for all to see. To illustrate how my whacky little mind worked even as a child of five or six, I remember thinking that there were likely more than a few individuals who, probably for exceptionally valid reasons, were very uneasy at the lack of 'natural' cover of foggy water and the resultant prospects of someone discovering what lay at the bottom of that lake. For a few days there was an assortment of people scurrying around, prodding the muck below their feet, studying each and every item retrieved from the bottom of that lake, probably for the exact reasons that I suspected, even back then as an innocent child.

It really is weird what one actually does remember, one of the things I remember the best was the horse drawn ice and milk delivery wagon. My recollection of details is fuzzy and I do not recall the actual man that drove the wagon but I do remember the horse. He was a pretty good size horse as I recall, however, when you are five years of age, any horse is a good sized horse! This horse was named was Bryce. We were constantly joking and chattering about Bryce's little fanny! Little fanny my rearend, that sucker was big! It is also awesome what one considers to qualify as good humor again when you're five or six years old. Other things that I recall are myself and my brother and sisters pulling our what we surmised as 'terrified' teddy bears around the house's semi-circular driveway, tucked tightly in cardboard boxes for their safety. We did this for hours and hours on end. It was sort of our own very dusty, very shoe destroying version of the Indy 500. I have a sneaking suspicion that Dorothy also did a few laps around that place with her 'Teddy' also, but we do not want to go in that direction, at least not in this book!

I also remember fishing for catfish with breadballs (no, the catfish did not have the breadballs, we did!) on hooks made from hand-bent sewing pins strung on sticks that we would get from the surrounding woods.

I have always suspected that we had in fact been 'sentenced' to Rawdon as unknowing accomplices for some unknown act against Dad. In any case, after Dad had decided that sufficient time had passed in the isolation of this particular wilderness wonderland and whatever sentence was to be served in Rawdon was either satisfied or stayed, the family was promptly moved to Montreal proper.

CHAPTER 6 – THE WESTMOUNT YEARS

Maybe Dad did have a heart. Maybe, even more likely, he had simply suffered a temporary fit of guilt and actually felt sorry for us kids being so isolated from the real world. Who knows, maybe he even felt sorry for Mom and her plight. He should have felt guilty, plenty guilty, after all, it was he that had 'sentenced' us to living life in its emptiest state, in the cool isolation of rural Quebec, La Belle Province of Canada.

With all of the retro-gratitude that one can possibly muster up, I have to say that, at least for my family's sake, I truly thank God for the intervention. I think he must have stepped in and made Dad relent and give in to a more humane treatment of his own precious family. It also may have been as simple as some personal or corporate decision that he would be perceived in a better business light if his family were closer and at least visible. Regardless of the reasons, we were in line to be reintroduced back into society in a far less hostile environment, one where we could do normal things and actually talk to most people in our native English tongue. Our reintroduction to society took place in the beautiful city of Westmount, Quebec, a bustling part of the actual city of Montreal. This section of the city is situated at the very base of Mount Royal, the famous inner city mountain with its giant illuminated cross which has become one, if not the focal point of the city and visible for miles at night. Westmount is a very upscale part of the city, and a most desirable place to live in most cases. To us, it was a step closer to Paradise where there was noise, traffic, stores galore, street cars and lots of people, we were back into the real world, sort of.

After the family banishment to Rawdon, Quebec experience I am sure that Mom would have agreed to move just about anywhere else and as for us kids, certainly my older sisters were more than ready for a move back into society.

Dad, probably with ample assistant from his young Girl Friday, actually I suspect she was Girl Everything, Dorothy found yet another house for us that had the ability to leave an indelible mark, not a positive one either, on any sane being's brain, especially a young impressionable one like mine. This place was an old duplex in Westmount.

In retrospect, I honestly and truly feel now that the choice of Westmount was more resulting from the fact that it was in close proximity to the infamous Allen Memorial Institute at the Royal Victoria Hospital, that very institution chosen and funded by the American Government's own CIA to allow the continuation of the horrific Nazi human experimentation programs under the covert tutelage of Dr. Death himself, Joseph Mengele. These horrendous LSD-based 'MKULTRA' and 'Monarch' mind-altering and psychic-driving experiments focused in part on unsuspecting family members of American businessmen living in Canada, the exact group in which our family was the perfect fit, again I digress.

Getting back to the house, the whole place was decorated in a fashion reminiscent of a very 'tacky' funeral parlor, very, very tacky and also very, very freaky indeed. I was six or seven years old by then and to me it was more than plenty weird. It was somewhat bizarre enough to have an impact upon me that actually eliminated almost any and all recall of the entire time I spent at that house as well as most events in my life during that time. On a more controversial note I honestly suspect that the aforementioned clandestine CIA/Nazi experimentations at the Allen Memorial indeed did play a pivotal role in my absence of memory.

Aside from a few casual and really unimportant details, I have almost no recall of events and happenings during the entire time that we spent at that house. I can recall most things that happened to me before we moved there. I can also remember most things that took place after we moved from there. For that period of time that we lived in that house, however, I have little recall.

Even the normally memorable 'milestone' events in one's life, especially when you are six or seven years old are non-existent in my mind. Things like the first days of school should really stick with you forever, but in this case they are not there leaving little more than a blank space in my brain.

I don't know whether it was the regular visits by the owner of the house, a weird old lady named Annie, the furnishings or the house itself, but the portion of my brain responsible for recall of that period of time was rendered almost useless, semi-zapped! I recall only bits and pieces of the things I thought scary but, as stated above, many of the normal milestones in life I simply do not remember. It may well be that, at least in my mind there simply weren't any normal things that happened there!

Dad leased the house, the actual owner of the place was a rather frail old lady. She used to dress in a fashion, and here I have to be somewhat repetitive, she clad herself in a manner reminiscent of a walking funeral parlor, just like the damned house was decorated! I can summarize my interpretation of the entire Westmount period by saying that the whole thing was downright freakish. The house was freaky, the owner was freaky, everyone around was freaky, it was a totally freaky experience, I think you get my point.

To give you an idea of just how freaky this place was to me, my fondest memory of the place was the fact that within walking distance from our house there was a park on Mount Royal where we kids used to go and play. One of my best recollections of Westmount is that while we lived there a pedophilic child murderer/mutilator on the loose who was using that park to lure in and 'grab' his young victims, doing his 'thing' with them then strategically placing their cut-up remains around the park. Mom, I am sure with the best of intentions, used to make sure that little time went by without reminding me of these horrific events that took place right up the street from our house!

Regardless of the inherent dangers of not only getting there, we had to cross a few major well-traveled thoroughfares as well as avoiding those with less than honorable intentions who frequented the recreational areas, it was a pretty neat place. In the middle of the park was a man-made small lake or, dependent upon your personal views, maybe it was a large pond. in any case it was a nice place to go and watch the world go by even as a youngster.

In the summer the water was used mainly for bathing and in the winter, like all outdoor things aquatic in and around Montreal, it became an ice skating area. Aside from the swimming in the summer, there was a local model boat club. The members used to bring their wonderful model sailboats, beautifully painted and rigged like the real things, to the water, launching them, then sitting back and watching the gentle breezes guide them in a race against each other. It really was a neat place, and I liked it a lot, except of course for the psycho child killer that stalked his prey there, right where we romped and played!

There were all sorts of indications that Mom found this house just as freaky as I did. Up to the moment of her death, she was adamant that, during our stay in this house, she and I used to spend our time riding the streetcars, all afternoon, every afternoon! Now, I'm not the most intelligent person on the face of the earth, but I can assure you that if that were indeed true and Mom and I had been on the streetcars to the extent that she claimed, she would have been given a white coat with long sleeves and a room 'at the Inn'. As for me, I cannot for the life of me figure out why that part of my life is almost a total blank! It may be that it is best that I do not know what went on that turned my little brain 'off' for that time span! I think that the all-afternoon 'streetcar' thing again had more to do with the mind-altering work at the Allen Memorial Institute than anything else.

Now I just know that you are wondering what in the hell is going on with Dorothy? Well, I was young and do not really remember hearing or seeing anything of Dorothy in Westmount. Looking back, I now know for certain that she was very much in the picture, in fact, she was gaining in prominence with each passing day, or should I say night! She was there all right, we just didn't see her. I bet that she was kept busy working behind the scenes or, I imagine, under cover, like really under the covers. I also suppose that there had to have been some major negotiations between Mom and Dad regarding good old Dorothy, concessions that Mom unwillingly gave into, which ultimately regained our collective freedom back into a real society. In retrospect I can see that, just like in those bad old Joseph Cotton movies Dorothy, and her co-starring role in Dad's play on life, must have been used as a bargaining chip in offering Mom another shot at a somewhat normal life. Poor Mom, God bless her soul. When I look back and see the sacrifices that this lady made to keep the family together, I am simply amazed.

The real love of my life was then, and continues to be, cars. Much to my surprise I can actually remember the cars that we had when we were residents of Westmount, never mind any real milestone events. Thank God that I have full recall of all of the cars that have passed through my life for it gives me the ability to take a sort of mental vacation anywhere, anytime. I can even smell each of them! The whole story behind our cars and the actual trip from Cincinnati to Rawdon is a whole other story, one which is well worth of another chapter. The short version is that when we first moved up to Canada, we did so in a white Buick convertible and a yellow MG TD, a very small and at the time very rare sports car made in England. It was a really neat car with a reddish maroon interior. Dad was the official pilot of the MG, with Mom having the bigger, more family oriented Buick to drive and lest I forget to mention, we made the thousand mile trip with only one set of license plates and registration for both cars. Exactly how Dad got us through customs and immigration with no registration for the MG who knows, again it is probably best that we never really knew how! In retrospect, again I suspect that, for whatever weird and most likely very questionable motives, it was with some covert assistance from the both the US and Canadian Governments.

My first personal 'good news, bad news' experience came in Westmount. I recall one night Dad coming home and soon afterwards, just before dinner, secreting my brother and myself outside to the garage. He flicked on the lights in the garage and explained that our beloved MG was gone. It had been replaced by a brand new silver Jaguar XK120 roadster which sat directly in front of us. He asked if we wanted to hear the deep throaty sounds from the twin exhaust pipes, who in their right mind could refuse? He got in and fired it up. It really did sound magnificent. He then flung open the passenger door and said come on, let's go for a spin. Without any more coaxing, we jumped in. He put it into reverse, pulled out onto the street, and we roared off for an extended ride. That was Dad, whenever he got the impulse to do something it was going to get done. The 'good news' was that we were going for a ride in the new Jag, the 'bad news' was that dinner would have to wait. When we returned home after a few hours of cruising, even I could see that Mom did not share his somewhat cavalier attitude towards us just dismissing her more than laborious dinner efforts that night.

Even though the MG was a really neat and uncommon automobile for sure back then, a Jaguar, however, well that was an even more unusual and truly spectacular car. Later in life I would have another MGTD. The reality piece involving the ownership and reliance upon an MGTD for day-to-day transportation can best been summarized in Oscar Wilde fashion, old Oscar would have said in a snickering amused way "the only thing worse than not having an MG, is having an MG"! truer words were never spoken.

Much like when we were in the snowy confines of winter in rural Rawdon, the snowy boundaries of Westmount proved to be just as challenging and bleak during most of the winter. Aside from the increase in traffic and people in Westmount compared to Rawdon it was still a rough environment for kids. Also, as was the case in Rawdon, fortunately for us kids we had little idea of just how inhospitable the place was for no matter how cold or snowy it would get, we would go into our defiant cold-denial mode. We would simply don as many layers of movement-limiting clothing as we thought possible. We would routinely risk life and limb to frostbite and other various dangers in our dexterity-challenged layered clothes state. It would be forty-five below zero and we would be out there skating, tobogganing, or just frolicking in the snow and having a whale of a time. Without having to conduct tons of time and resource consuming research I can say with all certainty that cold temperatures definitely affect the brain and how it processes the environmental effects on people, especially young kids.

We would go through sheer agonizing pain for hours and hours afterwards as a result of the exposure to the weather. We would go through the necessary contortions to assure that our frozen little hands and feet were able to get under cold running water. We would go through this in a very serious attempt to reverse the obvious frostbite and, of course, the resultant gangrene that we were warned would with all certainty set in forcing the amputation of our limbs, at least that was the constant admonition offered up by the grownups!

One of my very first lessons in the actual risk/reward 'thing' was taught to me while in Westmount. Montreal was in a snow belt and, being an island in the middle of the St. Lawrence river only exacerbated the condition. Being a major city, snow removal was a constant problem with on-going attempts at a solution. When it would snow, they would simply plow the streets so that the snow would get pushed out of the street itself and off to the side where it would pile up. Adding to the problem was as people shoveled their sidewalks and driveways, even more snow would accumulate on the edges of the streets. At some point in time these snow banks had to be removed and the city was well equipped to handle this with their fleet of huge snow bank chomping, snow-blowers. These were very large, truck-like vehicles with a contraption on the front that was around eight feet across and five feet high. There contraptions housed two huge fast-rotating augers that, when pushed into a snow bank, would chew through anything and everything in their path and send it up the connected spout into a truck which moved slowly down the street beside it. When there was a severe blizzard, they would simply move these beasts up and down the streets, eating through the snow banks and shooting the snow onto the yards lining the streets, not perfect but at least the traffic could move along the streets.

The resulting snow banks presented a very much-appreciated opportunity for amusement, at least to us kids. After all, these snow banks were there, and we were there! Obviously there had to be something that could be done to them that would allow us to occupy our time having even more fun in the frozen 'tundra'.

I am not certain, but I believe that there may well be one of those unwritten government mandates that requires among the very first things that you must learn about in Canada is the lifestyle and survival techniques of the Inuit, the North American Eskimo. I suspect that there is some type of Eskimo Lifestyle Teaching 'Police' that roam freely throughout the Canadian communities looking for those irresponsible parents who shirk this social obligation and do not teach their children how to make an igloo at the very earliest age. These teachings had to be done with the prerequisite of making sure that every member of the teeny-tiny little audience did not go more than a few moments without fearing imminent death from some uncontrollable cause.

The accompanying caveats concerning the very real, and very great potential for a cave-in of the igloo, must include warnings of the resultant excruciatingly painful, agonizing, drawn-out suffocating death. It was no different in our house. Building dwellings out of frozen blocks of snow, and tunneling into large piles of snow were taught to us as well and, we were also given the recommended daily allowances of death warnings should we do it wrong or, simply stay in there too long. My question to this day is what is too long? Is death really the first clue?

Anyway, with warnings firmly in our mushy little minds we would grab our shovels, run outside, and start digging into these snow banks in a passion seldom seen. We, of course, were clad in layer-upon-layer of our winters best, looking very much like multi-colored, over-stuffed badgers. Ultimately, we would end up with something that had one similarity to a real igloo, it was cold! These works of art were sort of a very, very poor man's version of an igloo but with all the warmth, elegance, and inherent suffocating dangers of the original. The real danger of igloos in the city we were soon to find out, would be most unfortunately demonstrated to us 'innocents' through a most horrible accident.

The awesome insulating qualities of well-compacted, thick snow walls is only outdone by their ability to keep sound out. When you were inside your frozen fortress, the rest of the world was all but gone. You could not hear your mother screaming at you for lunch or dinner, you could not hear passing traffic and, as we were soon to see, you could hear those awesome snow-blowers approaching.

We were not alone in our quest to build these rather awesome snow bunkers. There in fact was another kid right up the street from us that had excavated his igloo into the snow bank and was inside enjoying the spoils of his efforts. Unfortunately, the city had decided to remove the snow banks that afternoon and had brought in the awesome but potentially lethal snow-blowers.

I would imagine that this poor kid never had a chance. I remember seeing the red smattering on the snow in his front lawn. It was the first and only sign that the poor driver of the snow-blower had that the poor kid was even in there. It was the very last time that I ever dug into a snow bank in Westmount. I sat back and let everyone else do it, waiting patiently on guard to warn the others of the approach of those damned 'killing' machines!

We lived in that house for a period of a year or so, I really don't remember how long it was. Once again and for whatever reasons it was time to move the family on. Dad, I am sure with some input from Girl 'Everything', had picked out a new house for us, his most precious offspring. The house was in a small village named Senneville, a sort of suburb of Ste. Anne de Bellevue, which was a little city on the very western tip of the Island of Montreal, some twenty miles or so from the city proper.

CHAPTER 7 – THE SENNEVILLE HILLBILLYS

Again, for reasons probably best unknown, possibly but not likely out of the goodness of Dad's heart or, most likely prompted by more nefarious motivations, time again came to move the family out of the actual city of Montreal. Dad (maybe with help from girl Friday through Thursday Dorothy?) had picked out a new house in a small village named Senneville, sort of a suburb of the small city of Ste. Anne de Bellevue, itself a hamlet of the city of Montreal.

Ste. Annes was located on the very western tip of the Island of Montreal some twenty miles from the city proper. If there were a list of best places to live in the 50s and 60s, I am quite certain that Senneville would not have been ranked in the top 1000. Perhaps it would have made a list of the top 5000, just before Cincinnati! Now having said that, Senneville was the actual chosen place for Christopher Plummer to reside as well as the town in which the original movie 'The Fly' was supposedly based in. When we moved to Senneville in '53 or '54, our family was one of the two or three English speaking families there! If that were not bad enough, not a single one of us could speak any French! Sign language was in order. The first, easiest and most widely used sign word by us in Senneville was a hand wringing motion, this of course meant COLD! It was a very, very useful gesture, almost all year round.

Mom was solely responsible for the unbelievable 'en mass' learning of English by most of the locals. Mom was especially impacted by the language barrier because she truly seemed to have had an authentic 'mental block' disallowing her to learn any French. I really think, however, that my mother's perceived inability to learn French was in actuality the combination of her intelligence working in a concerted effort with her stronger desire not to learn French, ever, never! No kidding, thirty plus years later, pretty well every single person in Senneville could converse in English and speak it well, almost perfect, while Mom on the other hand could not, or should I say would not, even say oui (sounds like WEE Mom)! Go figure.

A great example of Mom's inability to retain anything to do with the French language is the 'Deer' story!

One of my sisters had a friend who was a local French Canadian who was also quite fluent in the English language. Now we had been surrounded by French speaking people for years by the time this story takes place. It was winter time when this fellow came to our house. We all sat around chatting when this fellow began telling us that when he was coming in the driveway he had seen a lot of deer piste all around the house and in the yard. The French word for tracks is 'piste'.

He then went on to say that it had to be a rather large deer, probably more than a hundred pounds and that, according to the size of the 'piste' it was most likely a buck, again in his opinion according to the size of the 'piste'. Mom sat there attentively and then blurted out in a somewhat surprised tone "you can tell all that about the animal from that deer piss?"

See what I mean about Mom and the apparent inability to digest anything in the French language.

The invasion of Senneville by our 'clan' must have been one awesome spectacle for the locals to experience and an entertaining one at that, The Canadian version of the Beverly Hillbillys was born!

The Senneville Hillbillys show came complete with six kids with another 'bonus baby' soon to be arriving, a constant gaggle of very strange 'foreign' visitors, a bunch of cars ultimately outnumbering the inhabitants of the house, lots of guns with more than ample amounts of ammunition, lots of noise making devices, and most importantly, loads of money and the innate ability to tastefully flaunt the same. As if this were not enough, a large, rather noisy, often-times cantankerous and free-wandering Great Dane was added to the mix. The locals may not have been the sharpest group in the world, but they did possess an uncanny, almost innate ability to sniff out money, and find a way to quickly accommodate those who possessed it. I believe that this 'prenez l'argent' (grab money) thing was a crucial component in Mom's apparent inability to pick up French, she quickly came to the realization that if you had money, and the locals had stuff to sell and needed the money, your need to speak anything other than English became moot.

The locals unintentionally became privy to serious ongoing recreational and sporting activities by our family and the many followers. Many of these events were based on our familial inbred 'need for speed'. These exercises were totally alien to those lesser local mortals but, none-the-less, over-the-top entertaining. Many of these pseudo-sporting activities required substantial amounts of skill, even greater quantities of bravery and, if possible, a far superior mixture of sheer luck and absolute, unadulterated stupidity. Our family was way, way ahead of our time in the performance of absolutely death-defying stunts involving an unbelievable assortment of motorized and non-motorized 2, 3 and 4-wheeled vehicles and other danger-laden human carrying creations and mediums.

The house was surrounded on three sides by a large verandah. The distance between the verandah floor and the ground ranged from about two feet to about six feet due to the changes in elevation of the yard. We always had an assortment of bicycles around. When I think back, there must have been weekly deliveries of bicycles as a result of our family's ability to destroy them. One of the main methods of bicycle destruction was our version of the Schwinn slam! We used to take the bikes up onto the verandah and line up on the side that led to the largest drop-off. When we felt the timing to be right, we would peddle as fast as we could and go hurtling off of the end of the verandah, resulting in spectacular 'crash and burns', bent and broken bikes as well as equally impressive bruises and painful injuries!

We also seemed to have access to other items that seemed to just be there for no other reason than to spawn questionable and rather dangerous activity. One of these items was a very large inner-tube from some industrial or aircraft application. Dad had brought this inner-tube home for us to enjoy and enjoy it we did! Our house was on the lake side of the main road. On the other side of this road, about one-half mile directly behind our house was a large hill. The hill was probably 200 feet high and was covered with a lot of vegetation ranging from thick, heavily spiked bushes to large, mature trees. There was, however, a natural open path down the front of the slope and in winter this hill made a great ski hill.

Our daredevil upbringing made us kids absolute experts in finding anything that could be used to get us from the top of that hill to the bottom in the shortest time at the highest rate of speed! Any off course excursion would result in dangerous, blood-letting collisions with the trees, rocks, bushes and other solid obstacles. Toboggans, sleds, large serving trays from hotels which were my personal favorite, cardboard boxes and occasionally after heavy sleet storms, ice skates.

To the amazement and absolute amusement of the locals we would navigate this hill with the greatest of speed. The summer presented another challenge, the hill was still there with its inviting slope, however, the natural slipperiness of snow and ice was gone. We occasionally ventured up with bicycles, but even us kids, as reckless as we were, did have some common sense and knew when to say no! Let us not forget that there was that inner-tube that Dad had graciously handed over. This thing had an outer circumference of about five or six feet when pumped up to about fifty pounds pressure! More importantly, the 'donut hole' in this baby was about two and a half feet in diameter and the valve stem was right in the center, it was bent at an angle, like a handle and it was actually large enough to really grab on to. We used to take this tube up to the hill, somehow get into the center opening, hang on to that stem for dear life, and then we would go down the hill.

This tube would jump and bounce its way down the hill gathering a great rate of speed on the way down, normally into the damned trees! Occasionally it would actually make it to the field at the bottom of the hill without spitting out and depositing the semi-dazed rider somewhere in between. We would normally be helped home by the befuddled but none-the-less highly amused locals.

We were always doing something 'outside of the norm' but out of all of the recreational sporting activities that we regularly engaged in, perhaps my personal favorite was *winter road surfing*. To perform this sport right there were certain absolute requirements. Warm clothing, thick, very thick-soled boots, good dry gloves, clean fresh icy roads and the key ingredient which was speed. The clothing was an anytime thing in the cold but the requirement of fresh icy roads meant that this sport was one of pure weather-related opportunity, as the snowflakes flew and the roads became really treacherous and, of paramount importance, before the sand truck had their chance to ruin the 'track', that's when you had to go and go we did. I guess you're wondering about the speed part. Well, the speed came from the passing cars and the local bus than ran the route every hour or so. The bus was the favorite 'ride' for you knew you could ride the diesel smoked Ste. Gennevieve 'Pipeline' for miles and miles! This event ran along Highway 78 which was a main thoroughfare with two narrow lanes twisting through the countryside. This route had a couple of great hills that were long, very curvy and, just to add to the challenge, full of potholes. There was also a great assortment of other dangerous obstacles, hindrances and hurdles. It was an awesome sport indeed and I miss participating in it to this day!

Ice, and frozen lakes to be more specific, as unpleasant and uncomfortable as they were, offered up an absolutely unlimited array of entertainment opportunities if one is able to forgo the necessity of human beings to retain body temperatures above the freezing point.

The combination of vast areas of slick, slippery, smooth surfaces and speed made the ability to get close to the 'edge' easy indeed.
Lest you think that summer was void of our treacherous personal exploits it was not. Summer allowed for another dexterity challenging, life-threatening display of sheer common-sense defying, circus-like up-in-the-air activities. The house was an old two story structure with a very steep shingled roof. There was a large dormer that jutted out from the roof that housed a balcony. This dormer was about thirty or thirty-five feet above ground level and the roof on the dormer was also very, very steep. Like most roofs there was a metal flashing, a very slippery flashing that separated the dormer roof from the main one on the house.

We kids saw this as nothing less than a magnet, attracting us to its ability to further test our survival skills. We would routinely go up to Jackie's room and head out onto the balcony. We would then take off our shoes, an imperative step in the so-called 'slide for life', actually the quick descent on the flashing. Sorry, I am ahead of myself here. With nothing but wool socks covering our feet we would carefully crawl over the railing and even more carefully, stabilize ourselves by placing a leg on each side of the slippery flashing then waddling up the roof to where we could relax 'on top of the world', straddling the peak!

It was more than just dangerous, it was dangerously exhilarating and like the excitement one gets from a terrorizing roller coaster, you just couldn't get enough! The ascent was actually a piece of cake, it was the 'slide for life' that was really the actual death-defying feat. We would carefully, and I do mean carefully, crawl backwards, downward on our bellies, until we felt the roof of the dormer with our feet. We would then very, very cautiously turn on our backs and slowly sit up. Carefully and with minimal movement we would place one foot in front of the other on the, yes I know it is repetitive, very slippery flashing then, in an act of sheer unadulterated stupidity, we would then 'push off' sending our innocent little bodies sliding down the flashing with one, and only one, way to safely terminate our death-defying downward plunge and that was to quickly and safely grab the balcony railing as you sped by! Luckily none of us missed the railing, there were a number of near misses which would evoke nothing but laughter from the rest. To miss that railing would have absolutely resulted in nothing less than death!

What was the main motivation for us kids to again risk actual life and limb on the roof? To get a better look at the stars, why else....duh!

I often look back and, in respectful retrospect, I have come to realize that Mom had to have known what we were doing. Why on earth could she have allowed such life-threatening activities? Hell, it was probably the aforementioned Cincinnati thing! Besides, why not allow us kids on the roof, we were allowed to get in gunfights on the front lawn using, and I'm not kidding, live ammo!!! I remember hiding behind 'Pirate' tree, a super-wide, large Oak while the bullets, pellets and darts would be whizzing by my head! Wow, how lucky were we? We obviously had our own version of a final police school training sessions. Maybe Mom recognized our ability to effectively deal with real danger. She obviously was just making sure that we all were fully prepared for life, after all, you never know when you will be shot at.

On a lighter note, I clearly remember playing outside in the yard as a young boy and seeing Mom through the large kitchen window, standing at the sink preparing food, getting ready to cook her heart out as usual. She certainly looked happy but then again what-the-hell did I know back then. We all seemed happy and I honestly think we were but, for the life of me, I cannot figure out why. We certainly did not have anything even remotely approaching a so-called normal lifestyle. To be honest when I think back all I can say is thank God!

We seemed to be more like celebrities than neighbors in our community and we certainly came to the fore and we all played this part up to the absolute max. This quite often was much to the detriment of many of the locals. There were others however, who relished our antics, they found themselves thoroughly entertained and amused at our family's ability to defy and circumvent just about all of the social, legal and environmental guidelines of the 'Great White North'.

One of the reasons why I wonder about our family's past happiness is that we were in reality a totally Fatherless household. To say that Dad was not home very often is a grossly modest understatement! I recall an incident when I was nine or ten years old, my brother George was thirteen or so. The house in Senneville was a splendid old thing and the yard was very large. There was an abundance of clustered bushes separating certain areas. We used to have a small tent and assorted camping equipment and George and I used to spend some weekend nights camping within the confines of these clusters in the yard.

George and I had some friends that we had been chumming with for a year or so. One of these kids was named Kenny who was also a very strange kid so we all got along fine. Kenny actually spent more time at our place than he did at his own home. One night George, me and Kenny were camping out in the yard. It was about three in the morning and we were into our fourth or fifth pot of tea. Sterno stoves were the rage at the time and ours was used to its full extent during these stays in the far wilds of the yard. We were engaged in some deep conversation when to our amazement the side of the tent began to flicker and then glow. The source of the light was the headlights of a car slowly coming down the driveway. The distinctive burbling exhaust note of the Corvette gave away the fact that Dad had arrived home from a trip to who knew where.

The car came to rest at the foot of the verandah steps where he extricated himself from the car and quietly closed the door. Upon seeing the dim lights of our tent he made his way over to us. He stuck his well-tanned, well-groomed head through the opening and asked if he might join us for tea. Dad always looked as though he just fell off of the Big Screen. He carefully shifted in and sat down. He was dressed in a suit, shirt and tie, polished shoes, the full nine yards. We talked and joked around for an hour or so after which he said he had to leave to get some sleep, then he was gone. A few moments passed and Kenny looked very puzzled indeed. He then looked at George and asked "who was that guy?" After a whole year, he had never seen Dad!

Dad indeed was a character and a half and then probably at least three halves more. Looking back now, he most definitely was more strange than comical. The iceberg theory of only seeing one tenth would probably be in order here for I'm sure that the vast majority of evidence of strange behavior lay well hidden under the surface, never to have been seen or noticed by other than those very close to him.

Absolutely no human was immune from his warped, weird, borderline-dangerous, but almost always entertaining sense of humor, again Dad was of German ancestry so the 'chadenfreud' thing was probably pivotal. Dad had many a strange fetish I'm sure, but one which became apparent on numerous occasions was his fascination with masks and the fine art of disguises.

Dad's vehicles of choice were convertibles. He always had a couple of convertibles for his own use, no kidding, and in all but the most horrendous weather he always had the top down. Sunshine, rain or snow, hot or cold, he refused to put up the top. His main teachings to me regarding the pleasurable use of the automobile was to always have the top down and go as fast as you possibly could under any and all conditions. His thought process was that the harder it rained, the faster you should go in order for the laws of physics to take over and eliminate the rain from hitting you directly, it would simply go right over your head, then hit you from behind. His philosophy on speed was that it was a most precious commodity in life and you should get as much as you possibly could. He tempered that somewhat with the next teaching, given a car that was a standout, if you were reasonable looking and you were able to converse through intelligent verbal diplomacy with an officer of the law, you stood a lot better chance of getting off if you were traveling at a ridiculously high rate of speed rather than just ten or twelve miles an hour over the limit.

He always made certain that his cars were more than up to the task of going fast. I again use the plural form here purposely for Dad always had a multitude of spectacular cars for his own personal private use. He would spend days on end in his cars covering great distances at breakneck rates of speed. He carried at least one full face mask with him in his cars at all times. I should also mention that he always carried a full flask with him at all times as well. He would garner great pleasure from putting these hideous masks on backwards and then carefully study, in his rear-view mirror, the behavior of those people who found themselves innocent patrons of his impromptu vehicular theater. He would get the biggest charge out of this stuff. He also carried a real glass false eye with him which he would use to amuse himself and his chosen entourage at the expense of some unfortunate unsuspecting victim. He would carefully slip the eye into some poor slob's drink when he was relaxing at some bar, sorry, I again ramble off point.

Perhaps the greatest use of Dad's masquerading talents was on those all-too-rare occasions when Dad would actually come home. For some reason which is probably best left alone at this point, Dad always seemed to arrive home from his trips very late at night.

I am reminded of an occasion when he took full advantage of the total surrounding circumstances to demonstrate his love of the masks and disguises. To get the full comical impact of this questionable yet humorous episode, it is important that you keep in mind that we lived a very, very short distance from the Senneville Lodge, a veterans' of war hospital for the criminally insane! This hospital housed the worst of the worst! When all else would fail, you know electric shock therapy, lobotomies, etc. they would send these certified crazy killers to this facility. The security at this facility was more than somewhat lacking and, as a result, the community would be terrorized on a weekly basis by escapes of the inmates into the wooded confines of the surrounding yards, yards like ours!

The sirens would blare and the community would go into full, gut-wrenching, septic tank testing alert status. The locals would run around collecting the kids, getting them indoors and locking up everything that could be used to get in. They would remain in their cluster-horrification until the 'all clear' was sounded. Everyone was more than fully aware of the dangers posed by these unfortunates yet, there was little that they could do about it. These unfortunate, battle-crazed individuals were referred to by the locals as 'blues' because of the almost royal blue corduroy suits they were issued at the 'bin'. Even the 'blues' that roamed freely, yes I did say freely, in the community were very, very strange. That certainly should come as no surprise for there was but one and only one requirement for admission to this place of horrors, you had to be certified as, you guessed it, totally absolutely crazy! We would see daily parades of the 'blues' as these poor demented souls were paraded in front of the locals on the street, most of the 'blues' displaying a vast array of contorted, and oft-times highly offensive, positions and gestures.

I was very young at the time and at a very impressionable stage in life. This phase happened to coincide with my weekly introduction to Alfred Hitchcock and other purveyors of bizarre and weird things on the then new 'tube' or television. The weekly strange offerings of these somewhat demented producers did nothing other than fan the blazes of my already well trained and equally demented imagination. I really did not need any help from TV to see things in a really weird light.

OK, let us get back to our story. Our house was situated on a large lake and, as was common in the area, we had a rowboat to roam around the lake. Because of this there were always life vests and paddles or oars scattered around the verandah. I used to like laying out on the lawn after dark and gaze into the darkness of the sky looking for shooting stars. I always thought that the best time to do this was later at night, around midnight or so. To accommodate this activity, I sometimes would sneak out my bedroom window and climb down off the roof then lay out on the lawn. Most of the time either all of the others in the house would be sleeping.

This one night I lay there looking into the sky. It was not the best night for stargazing as the moon was close to full making it difficult to see all but the brightest of the stars. As I relaxed I heard the crackling sound of a car going over the pebbles in the driveway, thankfully it was Dad. He was navigating the driveway with exceptional care so he would not awake anyone especially, I suspect, Mom! He made it to the side of the verandah and stopped the car. I ran over to meet him. I always looked forward to seeing him for a host of reasons not the least of which was that he would always sit with me and recount his most recent outrageous adventures.

With Dad there were always plenty of tales to be told, and he would normally do so in a most exciting and interesting manner. I always thought that hearing him recount his tall tales was far better than going to a movie! That was true, he and his adventures were far and away more interesting than any movie could have been, and also far more threatening to my long-term well-being than any movie could have been!

After an hour or so of story-telling Dad said "let's have some fun!" He asked me to quietly gather up one of the grappling poles and a life-vest that were down by the boat and bring them up to the stairs where he said he would meet me. I went and got the pole and vest then brought them up to the stairs as quietly as I could. Dad came around the corner carrying his suit jacket and a full faced mask, I could see right away that this would definitely be a night to remember.
"Have there been any breakouts from the hospital lately, any sirens?"
I answered that there were always escapes and that the sirens were common place. He said "good".

Now remember we were but a mile or so from this 'loony bin' and there was a full moon 'a shining'. Dad started by tying the life-vest to the pole which was about ten or twelve feet long. Once that was done he carefully put his suit jacket over the vest and buttoned it up. He then placed the mask onto the top of the pole and said "follow me".

He then slowly went around the corner of the house stopping just below the windows of my sister's bedroom.
"Are you ready? he whispered "watch this". He then very quietly lifted the pseudo-mannequin on the pole so that it was about even with the window. He then stated banging the pole against the metal eaves troughs. God only knows what flashed through their minds, I suspect that just as Dad had planned they saw nothing but one of the escaped crazy lunatics on the roof just inches from their window.

The full moon and the background screaming and crying, well he did not let me down, it was truly awesome. Dad had again fulfilled his mission, at least in my weird, developing little psyche, he made life better and more frightening than any movie! Wow! This is the stuff that weird, wacked out, anti-social misfits are made of! Again I ask "why not me?"

Well, all was not lost on me for I must be somewhat 'cracked' after all. Looking back I actually found all of these strange, highly questionable family 'high jinks' not only acceptable and in some convoluted way sort of normal, at least in my mind, but absolutely entertaining and a great basis upon which to further develop my little psyche and build my future life. Go figure!

Do not be misled, not all was 'rosy' and not all of the memories of this period of my life were good ones. There were tons of family strife, believe me, having an 'errant' father, actually and more importantly a hyper-errant husband to Mom in Dad, certainly didn't help a bit.

To add a touch of class to this 'written series of words' I will again inject music. Between the multitude of death-defying activities I actually learned to play the trumpet while we lived in Senneville. In all honesty I should say that I *almost* learned to play the trumpet, having never quite mastered the instrument. Every week for a year or so Dad had arranged for a limo to pick me up at the house and drive me some twenty miles to the actual city of Montreal where I would get personal lessons from none other than the leader of the orchestra at the then very popular Bellevue Casino. Just to briefly revisit a previous chapter in this book the Bellevue Casino, I have recently learned, was in fact one of the main venues where the unsuspecting American businessmen would be 'blackmailed' into 'volunteering' their precious own family members into the CIA's infamous, horrendous MKULTRA mind-altering experiments, I am beginning to get a headache but again, I digress.

Being personally tutored by the awesome Mr. Cozy was a truly remarkable experience. Additionally, my personal 'chauffer', a strange German guy straight out of Nazi 'Central Casting' named Zimmerman, was also a whole deal on his own, probably, I suspect that with minimal research, would be well-worthy of yet another book. Regardless, the trumpet lessons are actually not what really 'sticks' in my mind about this musical interlude in my life. What stands out in my mind to this very day was an incident that taught me many, many things most important of which is that regardless of how much you wish, hope and pray, sometimes things are simply totally, unequivocally out of your control.

One night on the way back home from the city we were traveling along highway 2 in the big Chrysler limo. For some reason I chose to sit in the front next to the very strange 'Zimmy'. Running parallel to the highway are two sets of train tracks. It was snowing quite heavily and the wind was also blowing, swirling the snow into the air and making vision somewhat difficult. Far ahead was an approaching train, it's very bright headlight reflecting off of the wafting snow. I loved trains and would take full advantage of watching them whenever the opportunity presented itself, this was no exception. We were traveling at about fifty miles per hour so my wait would not be long. As I studied the approaching train I could faintly make out the profile of what appeared to be a woman and she appeared to be walking on the tracks directly in the path of the train. At the same instant Zimmy also saw the woman and immediately started blasting the car's horn in an effort to alert her as to the danger from the oncoming train. Then everything just sort of went into slow-motion, seemingly slowing down to an absolute crawl and we could do little more than stare helplessly at the train as it just got closer and closer to the lady on the tracks.

We could now clearly hear the train's horn blaring over our car's horn, Zimmy and I were both panicking, hollering and screaming desperately in the car at the lady to get the hell off of the tracks, to no avail, it was truly hopeless.

Just as we were within yards of this poor woman, right in front of us and directly in our view, the train, unable to stop in time, hit this poor lady! Everything went pink, literally, it was the most horrific sight that I have witnessed to this day. It took me months and months to redirect that image to a non fulltime part of my brain. Every time I closed my eyes for months that's all I could see, like I said it was absolutely horrendous.

Sometimes, most unfortunately, no matter how much you wish you could intervene, things really are out of your control, that was the lesson in life that was dealt out to me that evening.

While we are at it, you know, talking about death and the indelible consequences it can inflict upon people, especially young, impressionable ones, let's look at another impossible to remove memory from my 'sheltered' youth in Senneville.

The house lay on the banks of the Lake of Two Mountains, a sizable body of water and extremely deep in many areas, with often-times very erratic, dangerous currents mostly in the pre-freezing Fall season. These dangerous currents, unfortunately for many poor souls, coincided with duck-hunting season. Duck-hunting was a must for any living, breathing French Canadian male and they would come out of nowhere, their mandatory duck-hunting-hat covered heads popping up from the hundreds of even more mandatory duck-hunting 'blinds' that would suddenly appear floating everywhere along the banks of the entire lake. Duck-blinds were 'bastardizations' of the traditional, here I go again, mandatory 'Versheres' row-boats. These ultra-creative duck-hunters would cover these boats with all sorts of wooden structures supporting nets to which they would carefully attach tree branches, weeds, reeds, whatever they thought would make the poor ducks not see the absolutely obvious, a branch covered row-boat carrying over-clad passengers with silly hats holding an awesome and very heavy arsenal of lethal weapons stealthily floating on the lake!

These low-sided vessels were somewhat unstable on their own, but when you added somewhat top-heavy, visibility and maneuverability limiting structures they became totally unstable boats that could, and all-too-often would, very easily capsize. Now add a full-grown man suddenly standing up in the boat raising a heavy shotgun above his shoulders and you have the inevitable, a boat that would simply flip over depositing the far-too-over-clad occupants and all of their belongings into the depths of near frozen Lake of Two Mountains, I think you see where this is going.

I personally think that these duck hunters grossly underestimated their fine feathered prey. I think that the ducks had it figured out, whether through their own teeny-tiny brain power or simply through years and years of observation on the lake the ducks came to the realization that these 'Versheres' row-boats, when fully laden with the hunters and their cache of weaponry, were indeed death-traps. It is my opinion that the ducks would quietly sit in the reeds commiserating on their next moves after which they would draw 'straws', hey, they were right there. The losers would have to take some risks and would quickly and tactfully take flight right over the hunters' boats. They knew that this would cause the hunters to jump up in these incredibly unstable boats causing a disastrous capsizing and downloading of the hunters, sentencing them to near certain death. The ducks would simply regroup and rejoice safely in the weeds and wait for human reports on the body counts.

Regardless of the actual cause of the inevitable multiple capsizings, dead bodies being plucked from the dark, frigid waters of the lake were the duck-hunting seasonal norm in Senneville and the environs. Most of the bodies would be severely bloated and rotting from having spent days underwater, only floating to the surface after ample amounts of gas formed in their then defunct innards! Many had also been ravaged by the fish and other aquatic wildlife, excuse me, I'm feeling a little woozy, I think I have to use the washroom!

Without going into any more gruesome and questionable details as to why some of these unfortunates were retrieved in front of our house. More significant to this story is the fact that the summoned officials actually brought the dead bodies into a makeshift morgue to wait until more officials could do something else. Much to my mortification they decided that the temporary morgue would just happen to be our living room! Our living room, the very same room that otherwise was our refuge, our sanctuary, a place where we could always feel safe, no matter what!

I still remember the chills that would rush through my little body as I would subsequently lay on the very same rug upon which these dead bodies had reposed in their pre post mortem state.

As was the case with the funeral for 'Chuckles the Clown' on the Mary Tyler Moore show the annual carnage of hunters at the hands of these feathered little flying Gladiators brought out some comforting comedic relief.

There was a joke that was actually being bandied about regarding two duck hunters. It went something like this, Jacques and Gaston were in close proximity on the lake ensconced in their respective duck-blinds when Jacques wanted to see if Gaston had seen any ducks.
"Gaston" Jacques whispered.
"Qua?" (French for 'what')
BANG!

That sort of tells it all.

Looking back, my life in Senneville was quite surprisingly to me, nothing short of a truly great experience. The multitude of cars, our wonderful Great Dane Duchess, my little sister Debbie was born while we were there and who could forget Steve our gardener. Steve was hired by Dad and in a very, very Dad-like way, Steve was actually an inmate/patient at the abovementioned hospital for the criminally insane! Yes, our gardener, the man that was at the house almost daily... thanks a bunch Dad!

Like life itself unfortunately our life in Senneville had to end and did so in yet another surprising and mind-altering way for me, a psychological twisting conclusion that is covered in Chapter 2 of this book.

CHAPTER 8 - GOOD EVENING, AMERICAN STYLE!

My Mother insisted to her dying day that it was not a purposeful act of revenge. She said quite emphatically that it was quite simply an accident. Dad on the other hand was absolutely rigid in his insistence that it was not just an act of chance, it was not just a simple accident, it seemed to have been done with the malice and forethought of any first-degree criminal act. I have to admit that I personally lean heavily towards Dad's version. I too think that it was not an accident. Both Mom and Dad have sadly passed on, so now we will never know for sure.

Dad, at least in my opinion, was a true master at deciphering those situations in life that defy logical explanations. It was the middle of winter. It was bitterly cold, windy, and, oh yes, snowy. There was nothing different or special about the weather that was winter in Senneville. What was different, and very special, was that Dad was actually home! To say that Dad was not home very often would be an understatement of truly monumental proportions! Five or six times a year Dad would show up at home for a couple of days then he would be off to who knew for sure, supposedly on the road again for business reasons. When Dad was home, however, it was truly an event. When Dad would come home it was sort of an impromptu celebration of anything and everything. For reasons probably very relevant to this story, Dad would decide from time to time that it was time to share the wealth a bit with Mom. I suspect that the true reasons for these improvised handouts were rooted more in some sort of peace offering than in any true feelings of gratitude or generosity towards Mom. In any case Dad, a few weeks earlier, had arrived home with a new car for Mom. It was a nearly new 1952 Cadillac 4 door Sedan DeVille, shiny black outside and gray inside, a pretty nice car indeed.

With good reasons I'm sure, Mom showed absolutely no appreciation for either the gift of the car or, the car itself. In reality she clearly demonstrated a sort of arrogant disrespect for this massive black and chrome-plated monster. I sort of recall the very beginnings of this 'battle of the minds' about to unfold and be played out right in front of my little eyes, supposedly over this fine automobile but again I suspect that there was far more to it.

There were additional members of the audience, namely my sisters and brother who also were about to witness these mental maneuverings with me. The battle's first volleys were subtle, very subtle indeed. They were in fact offered with little in the way of detectable outward animosity, just an increasing series of somewhat subdued cerebral pokes and mental jabs in concert with slightly stinging 'combinations' at each other. Even with little to go on at that point my small but somewhat experienced little eyes and brain knew a battle was indeed already raging.

As the day drew on, the engagement slowly but surely escalated towards, then into the inevitable more open, more sensual type of confrontation so necessary for 'bragging rights' and to lay any claim to victory in the future.

The family was just finishing dinner when, sort of out of the blue, Dad announced that we had to go down to the village for something. He made it sound as though it was an absolute and immediate need, sort of an emergency without the panic component. Now keep in mind that it was well below zero, snowing and getting dark out. Not a good time for a ride for any reason, even a real emergency.

The mental jousting was in full gear and was really getting stoked as Dad again suggested that not only should we drive to the village, but that we go in Mom's new car! What was even a greater shot was when Dad suggested that this would be the perfect opportunity for Mom to drive her brand new Cadillac. She of course did the 'No' thing but to no avail as Dad again had her covered in that he then asked us kids whether or not we thought Mom should give in and drive us to St. Annes. Mom didn't have a chance. Mom was seriously outnumbered and worse than that, she knew that she had been outmaneuvered.

Before we could say that we were freezing our little butts off, we were packed into the frozen Caddy and on our way. Now Dad was never one to miss any opportunity and he recognized, and had decided to take full advantage of the situation that had presented itself in the necessity for him to show Mom how to operate this black behemoth. He was purposely speaking to her in monosyllables, simple little words, and for theatrical impact his words were offered in a condescending tone as though she had just come out of the backwoods of Arkansas. Just what we all needed at that point! In spite of Dad's most valiant attempts at tasteful mental bludgeoning, Mom, who also was able to recognize what was happening, was doing just fine having made easy work of the driveway. She now aimed the beast out and onto the main thoroughfare and was actually proceeding cautiously down Senneville Road, the main, actually the only road to the village. Mom retaliated by hitting the throttle just enough to get the rear end fishtailing. Our 'gang' of small captives in the back of the car were all very, very impressed indeed. I think we were all quite sure that the uneasy sliding from side to side was a well-planned and even better executed move by Mom in order to be assured of securing everyone's complete and undivided attention, it most definitely worked! I think we all knew that we were active participants, willing or not, so we simply let it go by and sat in the back seat hanging on paying strict attention and in a somewhat weird way enjoying the show.

It really was not a great night to be on the road for it was really terribly cold and rather difficult to see through the blowing snow. The icy roads as normal only added to the danger. The village of St. Annes was a few miles from the house so there was more than ample time for many strategic moves to be made in this questionable game that Mom and Dad were so intent on playing. Mom must have been in overdrive in the thought processes involving this engagement. She was working an impromptu strategy to eliminate whatever damage had been done to her position by giving in to Dad's incessant demand that she drive that damned car! She must have seen that whatever move she was going to make would certainly have to be one which would far outweigh her giving in to Dad. Mom must have seen that whatever she did next would have to be a move that would leave little if any doubt that she was committed to, and intent upon, becoming the ultimate winner.

The snow blew in grayish white sheets across the road as this private road show made its way past the Senneville police station that lay about mid-way between our house and our destination, the store in the village. The car's radio was on and Dad was sort of searching somewhat in vain for something other than the broadcast of the Montreal Canadians hockey game. About the only other program that I can recollect ever being on was a telephone request music show hosted by a guy named Leo Lachance. I'm quite sure that Leo would be overwhelmed if he knew that someone other than his relatives, some sixty-plus years later, would remember him or his show!

There were only three or four stations in the area but Dad continued the search as well as the strategic baiting of Mom by suggesting things such as the speed at which she piloted the car was somewhat excessive in light of such dismal driving conditions. Mom, I trust and hope, was doing her best to keep us all safe under the circumstances but on the surface appeared to be on the verge of something big, like losing total control! I could see a sort of semi-glazed glare in her eyes in the rear-view mirror as she took mental notes of all of the kids' positions on the rear seat. Mom also displayed a look of confident arrogance and also sounded rather confident. It's my bet that she had in fact already figured out what her next move would be and she was actually in the beginning stages of putting her next piece of the plan into action.

The road upon which we traveled, Senneville Road, comes to an end at St. Anne Street, there actually is a three-way stop at a tee and to add to the excitement there is also a slight dip before the stop. Oh yes, so that I do not forget any of the important parts of the story, there are also houses closely bordering both sides of the road approaching that point. The little hostages from their vantage point on the back seat could easily see that the end of the road fast approaching. About a quarter of a mile from this termination of the road is when Dad began showing some signs of weakening and was suggesting that any 'prudent' driver might very well begin to slow down for the fast approaching need to stop. This warning appeared to me to go unheeded for Mom showed no signs whatsoever of letting up on the gas. Another quick warning came and went with the same result. By now we were in reality much too close to the intersection for anything to happen that would be remotely associated with any version of a safe stop. We all began looking around, frantically searching for solid things to hold onto in the back of the big black Caddy. I thought to myself that at least the front seat-backs appeared to be soft and very well-padded so that they would minimize the final pain that we were all certainly going to feel as we met our maker in this black beast.

Another super-quick warning from Dad and a split second later Mom decided it was the exact right moment to deal her cards clearly, all of them right then and there! Without a word of warning she hit the brakes as hard as she could and we began a series of frightening gyroscopic spins and slides in the road that would have made Joey Chitwood proud. Because of the ice, we were not really slowing down as the car careened and bounced to and fro off the large icy snow banks that lined the road. Mom I believe was just waiting for that exact right second to make her move. I surely hope that Mom actually did have a plan and had decided that just for added effect, and to make sure that this maneuver in the battle had its full desired effect, she would score as many points as humanly possible in this situation. Just as the car was pointing towards a little house on the edge of the road she stood on the throttle 'big-time' and the car, with its little screaming occupants, took on a trajectory that propelled us directly towards, then right into one of the cute little houses that lined the street.

Now, it is important to remember that it was Saturday night, and it was a French Canadian village only a few short miles from Montreal and Saturday nights in Montreal in the winter could mean only one thing, Hockey! Anybody in and around Montreal that was worth his or her weight in snow was going to be watching Hockey Night In Canada with Foster Hewitt. The poor old man that was sitting in that house that lay in our path of destruction, much to his short-term misfortune, was no exception. It was awesome! The combination of metal bending, snow and ice sailing through the air, my sisters screaming, boards, bricks, stucco and dust flying everywhere, coupled with pure fear as we went hurtling into that old guy's living room was breathtaking. I can only imagine what this poor old man who was in his hockey trance must have thought! As I said, I thought that it was a spectacular sight for my adventurous little mind.

Well just as the dust was settling and the poor old man was

regaining his breath and concentrative powers, Dad emerged from the car, dusted himself off with all the theatrical prowess of Sir Lawrence Olivier, looked at the TV set for a minute or so then slowly turned to the old man and softly said "good evening sir, what's the score?"!

Dad was a really cool guy.... sometimes!

CHAPTER 9 – NEW YORK, NEW YORK, DAD AT HIS VERY BEST!

About the same time as Ian Fleming was putting 'pen to paper' creating Secret Agent 007 I actually had a like image in my young adolescent brain. I could see an international playboy type operating as a secret agent in an undercover world traveling the globe engaging in everything from espionage to murder to who knows what else, the 'agent' in my brain, however, was far more real in that it was my Dad!

It was in the mid-fifties, I was in my pre-teen years and for whatever reasons Dad decided that he would take only me with him on a so-called business trip to New York City, a pretty big deal at that age. I really do not know why I was the 'chosen one' but I do know that Dad almost definitely had a specific motivation in mind, he always did. Not only was I going to NYC with Dad but we were going to drive there in Dad's awesome brand new gun-metal gray Cadillac Eldorado convertible, what a ride.

With a couple of suitcases and Dad's familiar 'barn' shaped hand luggage stashed in the Cadillac's rather huge trunk we were on our way. It took a couple of days to get from our house outside of Montreal to New York City resulting from a stay-over in some hotel in some small city along the way.

It was always interesting and exciting to be with Dad whether it be his outrageous antics, normally at the expense of the unsuspecting, his hyper-educational conversations or, one must not forget, his unique driving style. Remember, back in the fifties most highways, including Highway 9 which was the main thoroughfare that you would take from Montreal to NYC, were simple two-lane roads, paved, but two lane none-the-less.

Two lane roads were perfect for Dad, the ultimate in road-racer wanabees! He loved driving fast, actually he really, really loved driving very, very fast. Driving at the outer 'limits' is great on a track where all other drivers are expected to be going in the same direction but in the real world of driving on a two-lane highway, slower traffic present a 'clear and present danger'.

I purposely have injected the legal term of 'clear and present danger', an idiom often used in courts during murder and self-defense cases because Dad, when confronted with slower drivers took on an almost diabolical attitude akin to someone being confronted with a situation that could easily justify inflicting death or debilitating injury on the offender. Night or day, rain or shine this slower car confrontation always ushered in nothing less than horrifying but hyper exciting automotive maneuvers that rendered any roller coaster ride a 'walk in the woods'! The resultant absolute terror from these masterful driving exercises was only exacerbated when you are in the front passenger seat having your forward view totally blocked by the offending car in front. Dad would quickly jerk the steering wheel to the left resulting in the car being flung out into the other lane and, of course, into the direct path of any and all cars, trucks, buses or any other on-coming traffic. Depending on whether there actually was on-coming traffic, and if there was what was the estimated time of impact, Dad would either fling the car back in or, even more frightening, stand on the throttle sending the car hurtling down the on-coming lane hoping to pass the miscreant, reprobate of a slow driving SOB before what would most likely be an excruciatingly painful ultimately fatal head-on collision! Well, I am writing this so obviously Dad's ability to use depth of perception and vehicular 'closing rate' estimations to his personal driving benefit was better than I imagined at the time. This rather unique ability was put to one other outrageous and very, very weird use by Dad.

Dad displayed many, many idiosyncrasies in his daily activities but one, while driving at night, one in particular would emerge, one which eclipsed all others by miles and miles! As I stated earlier Dad would risk life and limb to get buy slow-moving vehicles, slow-moving being defined by anything traveling less than absolute full-throttle, hyper-speed! Again remembering two-lane highway driving, there was one other situation that would render Dad into a maniacal, revenge-filled 'looney' and it would happen when there were no cars in his lane, just on-coming traffic, on-coming traffic that would not dim their lights! That was the problem. Dad's answer was exceptionally unique and very, very effective when done well. I have one additional reminder that I must inject here and now before I offer up Dad's solution.

Back in the day air-conditioning in cars was all but non-existent, people drove with their widows open.

Anyway, Dad's answer to the all-too-numerous non-compliant, non-dimming headlight scoundrels was the unpatented 'dog poop baggy'!!!! Yep, you heard me a plastic baggy, custom loaded with our wonderful Great Dane, Duchess's poop! When confronted with any on-coming driver not dimming their blinding headlights, Dad would simply reach down under the seat and retrieve one of the pre-loaded baggies and, using a combination of the aforementioned mental ability to rapidly determine vehicular 'closing' rates along with the ultra-rapid assessment of the physical dexterity needed to fling a baggy of that weight and size, he would wait until that exact essential 'let go' moment then, with accuracy worthy of any circus 'knife thrower', release the fecal-filled projectile into the offending driver's window, awe, whammy, the sweet smell of justice well served!

Ultimately we made it safely to NYC and Dad easily found his way to the renowned Biltmore Hotel, where we would stay in absolute luxury in a three room suite for the next four or five days.

The next morning we got up, got breakfast and was on to our first order of official 'business' was to stop at the Royal Bank of Switzerland and deposit the contents of Dad's 'barn-shaped' luggage, a cool couple of hundred thousand in cash! I was in total awe to say the least. That being said, however, that is not the main focus of my recollection from that day. What played a very pivotal role in my ultimate development was something much less outrageous that I had witnessed in a hallway at the hotel right after breakfast.

Dad had left me alone in the lobby to go and retrieve the 'barn' case from the room... yes, he actually kept it in the room, I guess so that he would not invite undo attention to it. As I waited I walked down a hallway off of the lobby where some artwork had been hung, even at such a relatively young age I was mesmerized by one of the pieces, it was a small, very simple watercolor work, maybe a square foot or so, of a single black oboe on a burgundy velvet background. It was striking, the detail was beyond anything that I had ever imagined could be accomplished in that medium. I'm not kidding, the artist somehow had infused unbelievable detail into the finished product that it was as if you could actually reach in and pick the instrument off of the velvet.

At the time that I actually first saw the painting I did not know what the instrument was, it was only when Dad brought me out of my pseudo-trance over the painting that he told me that it was in fact an oboe. He also was impressed with it to the point that upon our return to the Biltmore he inquired at the desk regarding buying it and, most unfortunately, was told that it had been sold earlier in the day.

I bring this up in this story because this book is supposed to give 'special' insight into the development of my psyche. It was that serendipitous viewing of that particular painting which instilled in me the absolute desire to somehow create that same dedication to detail as was in that painting. Many decades later I was finally able to successfully create fine line, ultra-detailed medical illustrations that reflected a level of detail that satisfied the desire to do so originating in my original viewing of that artwork in the hallway just around the corner from the famed clock at the impressive Biltmore Hotel.

The rest of the day was filled with going to different museums in the city where we would wander around looking at everything from a huge whale hanging from the ceiling to display after display of insects in glass cabinets. I only wish that I could go back and refresh my memory as to who else we may have encountered at these venues for I suspect that Dad may have had more going on than just showing me the unbelievable contents of these museums.

Another mind-altering experience came later that night when Dad took me to the Old Brauhaus, a large and very popular uber-authentic German restaurant in the city. It was more than just an extremely impressive reception for Dad when we arrived and walked through the old, large wooden doors. The lederhosen-clad band stopped playing immediately and announced to the substantial crowd that one of the owners had just entered... one of the owners! I had no idea that Dad was even involved in a restaurant, especially such an apparently popular institution. As though that surprise was not enough, during dinner the band leader, a rather rotund and very Germanic looking man named Brutus, asked Dad to come onstage and demonstrate his musical talents through a most difficult instrument to play, the violin. To my amazement Dad quickly obliged. His impromptu 'off-the-cuff' recital was nothing short of a 'virtuoso' performance with the violin not just producing music but, with Dad's skillful manipulation, the instrument seemed to sing to the entire audience with such emotion that it actually brought tears to the eyes of many of the patrons, both male and female. I can tell you it was one awesome experience!

The taxi ride back to the hotel was both interesting and educational with Dad explaining the popular history of the Brauhaus especially during the years of prohibition from 1920 to 1933 when the NYC police department routinely turned a 'blind eye' to the establishment continually doling out traditional German fare including of course, ample amounts of beer.

The next morning we got up early, had breakfast at the hotel then went off for another day of exciting surprises. Movie theaters, Automats, race car shops, nothing was off-limits. After an event-filled morning Dad flagged down a taxi and gave the driver an address. The trip took ten minutes or so after which the cab stopped in front of a theater, the famous Ed Sullivan Theater where we got out.
"Let's go see what's going on, he's usually doing rehearsals for his show."
We walked through the doors and into the lobby, I could hear someone singing within the theater itself. Dad said to be quiet as we made our way through another set of doors and down the central aisle to the base of the stage where the orchestra 'well' was.
"Guten tag Herr Mueller" (Good day Mr. Mueller) came from the well.
It was Brutus, the musician from the Brauhaus, he was part of the orchestra that played for Ed Sullivan's weekly TV show.

The singing had just ended as Dad and Brutus engaged in further conversation. The girl that was singing was a rather shapely, very pretty young woman who, upon hearing Dad's voice, came scurrying to the edge of the stage and started an "oh Georgie" thing with what I could tell, even at my tender, most innocent age, was somewhat sexual in its seductive delivery.

Within minutes we were all on stage where the Sherelles were warming up. Dad introduced me to the young lady who was sort of hanging onto him, actually they had engaged in a bit of an embarrassing, at least to me, lip-lock as soon as she was within reach! The young lady was an up-and-coming Broadway dancer and singer. Within another minute or so Ed Sullivan emerged from behind the curtains and, again to my absolute amazement, knew Dad actually calling him by name. Dad, of course, graciously introduced me to Mr. Sullivan.
"My son has been taking trumpet lessons" he blurted out "why not listen to him play." I was sort of mortified, I didn't know whether to run or just throw-up right there. I did neither and as Dad had done the night before politely gave in, how could I not?

Dad asked Brutus if he could fetch a trumpet for me and Ed and the gang just stood there waiting. Brutus emerged from the well with a well-seasoned 'horn' which he handed to me. I was trapped to say the least.
"Well, what are you going to play for Mr. Sullivan?" asked Dad.
The only song that I really had mastered, if you'll excuse the expression, was a contemporary trumpet standard.
"It's cherry pink and apple blossom white" was my response. With all the courage I could possibly muster I raised the trumpet to my quivering lips and began my trembling, ultra-amateurish, pathetic rendition of this not-so-wonderful classic. Out of the corner of my eye I could see Dad and 'tootsie' disappearing behind the curtains to no doubt engage in their own rendition of another human 'classic'.

All's well that ends well they say, Mr. Sullivan was most polite, actually standing there for the whole song but stopping well, well short of offering me a spot on the 'show', thank God. I should have been much prouder of my 'feat', how many people ever got the chance to personally play for Ed Sullivan? Again, looking back I suspect that I was little more than a 'pawn' to buy some time in

Dad's life-long personal 'tootsie' memory gathering game. I was most hopeful that all of the embarrassing, potentially humiliating trials were over.

Abercrombie & Fitch was a store situated right downtown NYC that, according to Dad was famous for always having at least one 'personal' submarine in stock. Why anyone in New York City would want or need a personal submarine still haunts my mind and, more to the point, why would Dad have any interest in these things? In any case we found ourselves in the store actually checking out one of these awesome submergible devices. After ample examination of this machine Dad said that he wanted to check out the assortment of rifles that they had. It was not uncommon for Dad to go on hunting trips including hunting 'safaris' for tigers and other big game in Africa and Asia. To engage in these expeditions required some exotic heavy-duty firepower.

We found our way to the gun department where Dad engaged one of the sales staff asking to see what they had for elephant hunting. The clerk said that they had a 300 HH Magnum that was guaranteed to take 'anything' down. Dad I recall was enquiring specifically about the velocity and the maximum range for target shooting. The clerk came back with some data as well as a 'scope' that answered Dad's queries. The gun was awesome as far as guns go, the stock was a multi-grained Weatherby, more of a work of art than a simple rifle stock. Dad bought the gun and a bunch of bullets which looked like small rockets to me. Dad then went down to the clothing department and bought a somewhat rigid suit bag in which he placed the gun. He explained to me that it would be a lot easier and raise far fewer questions if everyone, especially at the hotel, thought he was carrying clothing than if they knew he had this 'cannon'!

Back to the hotel we went, it was late afternoon by then and we went directly up to the room to take it easy before dinner. Back then air conditioning was rare indeed and hotels had windows that actually opened. Dad told me that he had reserved this specific corner suite on the upper floor of the hotel. It had plenty of windows which Dad had opened for fresh air.

Looking Back on a Warped but Wonderful Childhood

Two things remain in my brain about this one afternoon. As stated earlier, Dad always had a plan or some most often highly-veiled lesson in life to be learned from his actions. He called me to the window and started a verbal dissertation on wind currents, specifically in cities. He went to the desk in the room and got the small metal trash can which he then filled with a gallon or so of water and brought it back to the window. He said that it was about office closing time so that the sidewalks far below would be busy. Now he was going to demonstrate what he had told me about the wind currents and how they turn and wrap around buildings down town, altering everything in their path with somewhat predictable results. He lifted the trash can to the window sill and told me to watch the water as it went down to the ground.
"It will wrap around the corner of the hotel and land on the unsuspecting people walking below".

He slowly poured the water from the can, we watched from multiple windows as surely as predicted the water made the turn and indeed cascaded onto the unsuspecting pedestrians below. Dad sort of 'bellowed' in joy at his impromptu dousing of those folks on the street.

The second remembrance is even more questionable, troublesome and far more puzzling to me even as a kid. Dad was a bit of a stickler for time, sort of like the baseball player's wife in the OJ trial that, when pressed about being a 'stickler for time' by OJ attorney F. Lee Bailey, rolled up her sleeve producing at least four wristwatches attached to her arm!

Dad was always checking the time, this afternoon after our 'water redistribution' demonstration was fast approaching dinner time. Dad had opened the garment bag and taken the 'cannon' out and placed it on the bed. He then took one bullet out of the box, lifted the gun from the bed and with click inserted the bullet into the 'chamber'. The windows were still open and the drapes sort of fluttered in the breeze.
"Are you ready to eat?" he asked. My response was a definite yes.
"Good, get your jacket and we are out of here."
I went to the closet and grabbed my jacket.
"Don't you want to hear what this baby sounds like?" he asked as

he lifted the gun. I remember being somewhat reluctant to answer, I had heard plenty of guns and to fire that thing in the room would definitely create some issues, I addressed my concerns.

His answer was that if the muzzle of the gun were far enough out of the window and the other windows were closed the boom of the gun would be heard only from the outside. He then went and closed all but one corner window and got the gun. I remember Dad taking his time, looking intently through the scope of the rifle and then a rather large explosion from the gun.

Dad very, very quickly slammed the window shut and with no wasted time stuffed the rifle between the mattress and springs, grabbed me and ran from the room, locking the door behind us. We were well on our way to dinner as the questions as to what the hell had happened must have started being asked. We stayed out late and there were absolutely no questions or concerns raised as we got back to the hotel. We checked out and left for home early the next morning.

Dad was an expert marksman and a very intelligent person. He certainly was fully aware of the inherent dangers of shooting a firearm in any city, especially a city like New York. More troubling is the fact that he knew the dangers of an errant high velocity bullet in an area that is very highly populated, innocent people could easily get killed.

With the abovementioned knowledge I often, to this very day, think that it was very unlikely that Dad would purposely have endangered innocent people through such an irresponsible act, much to my mortification it is far more likely that Dad in fact had a specific target in his sights! I trust that I am wrong on this one but again, most unfortunately, we'll never ever know.

CHAPTER 10 – GRAMP'S WEIRD SCHOOL OF HARD KNOCKS - 'THE POT OF SOUP' THEORY!

Grandpa Mueller prized himself on his ability to cook, I am quite certain that he saw himself as nothing less than a Paris-trained chef. He was in fact a pretty good cook, but most certainly not a chef. To be more accurate, the proper description of Grandpa's culinary talents would have been that he was a fantastic *camphouse* cook, sort of the modern version of the old Western 'chuck wagon' master. He could take questionably edible things of a chewy or gooey consistency, that would otherwise be considered of absolutely no value from the standpoint of the traditional culinary arts, combine it with more acceptable ingredients, and make an acceptable meal out of it. He would sort of marry them together in a pot (the word *cauldron* is probably far more appropriate) with the other lesser desirable goodies and come out with a pleasantly palatable combination of rather delightful chomping and chewing. A camphouse cook extraordinaire to be sure, chef, I don't think so! Another benefit in his favor was the fact that chow time was normally after either a long period of hunger building rest, or a period of heavy labor. This probably accounted for a great heaping helping of the palatability of his culinary creations.

Grandpa also saw himself as somewhat of a teacher. He was an unlicensed instructor in the fine art of getting through real life, specialized in one single, simple area, that being all things covered under the word 'everything'. In almost anything that Grandpa did, one could find a host of hidden teachings. Grandpa was surely the forerunner of 'Master Po' the real main character on the popular television series Kung Fu. Master Po was forever testing his young students in life with well-founded, but most confusing, confounding, veiled lessons that for decades would go unrecognized by the students as actual teachings to be learned. It was only after some huge tragedy, or traumatic experience, that the students of old would realize that which had been taught decades earlier.

There were some lessons, however, some of the most valuable of all lessons to be learned from this simple looking, but very complex, elderly gentleman. In fact the very first lesson that would become clear was that the easiest way to avoid trouble was that, under no circumstances, should one ever emulate, or do what he did, in the manner in which he did it. There was always a shorter, less painful, and above all else, a better way of doing anything that Grandpa did! His ability to utilize his questionable talents for teaching was really quite incredible. After only a few hours in his informal institution of higher learning, your mind would be trained to systematically evaluate what you were being told as to its truthfulness, the methods, and the reasons for doing it in the first place!

Now let's get on with this story. I awoke one morning at the Lodge to the smell of coffee and the clatter and clanging of mettle, a very loud thud, a series of grunts and groans intermingled with some good old fashioned cussing and swearing. When at the Lodge I used to sleep in the loft above the kitchen area, so it was not unusual to be awoken by someone moving around below, but this morning was far noisier than any normal routine. Sensing something wrong, I jumped from the bed and perched over the side of the loft and peered down. I saw Grandpa, in a rather dazed, glassy-eyed state, lying on the floor, muttering obscenities surrounded by a number of large, mettle cooking pots and, a broom. The pots were normally hanging above head level from a large device that was attached to the ceiling of the kitchen. Most were still there, but there were a couple of empty spots. After inquiring as to Grandpa's physical condition, he said that all was fine and that it was just a little accident. Grandpa was not a big man. Dad knowing that most people, including his father, would be unable to even think of reaching the pots, saw fit to put a couple of small foot stools and ladders in the kitchen area. They were put there so as to accommodate the exact thing that Grandpa wanted to do, that being to get the pots down from the hanging device. Grandpa, in his infinite wisdom, felt that to seek out, and more importantly, to use these stools and/or other devices to mechanically lift him to a more appropriate level was, well, a simple waste of energy. Instead he had concluded that a common broom handle would be a much more efficient method of retrieving these somewhat weighty pots. More efficient? No way. Quicker? You bet! I don't know how he was not seriously injured because one of the pots weighed a good five or ten pounds!

A little dazed, but no worse for-the-wear after this first miscue of the day, he got up and said,
"Ajax (that was just one of the many nicknames that he and Dad had given me), do you like soup"? I replied that I, in fact, was very fond of soup, I liked it a lot.
"Good, then hurry up and get down here then, we got some soup to make".

I got dressed quickly and climbed down the ladder into the kitchen area. Grandpa then asked, "What kinds of soups are there, you know, what should we make?"
Now I was only a young lad of thirteen or so, but I knew something about soup. I replied that there was tomato soup, chicken soup, beef soup, ox tail soup, barley soup, the list went on and on.
"No, you're wrong" he quickly said "there is only bad soup and good soup, and we are going to make some really good soup"!
Then he asked,
"What flavors of soups are there?"
Now it was time for my display of soup knowledge, so again I repeated the list of types of soups. Even at the tender age I could sense that there was going to be more to this soup-making episode than simply making soup. He asked what my favorite soup was, and I answered chicken. Grandpa then went into a lengthy dissertation about the fact that chicken soup was by far the easiest to make as a result of the chicken having so much fat and skin that when cooked with anything else it masquerades their flavor.
"Even a bad cook could make good chicken soup" he exclaimed, I think it was strike one for me. He then went on to say that there was far more challenge in making good beef soup. It required a greater degree of skill in picking the right combination of ingredients, especially in the selection of bones for the stock. Also, unlike chicken soup with which everything goes, one had to be far more discriminating in this choice of ingredients resulting from the inability to match beef with many culinary offerings.

He then suggested that we sit down and methodically plan out our 'soup adventure' as a precaution against doing something unintentional that would compromise what should be a spectacular event for the palate. We sat down at the counter and he started asking what I thought would go well in this soup. As I made suggestions, he would either accept the suggestion with an acknowledgment of the choice, or, he would reject the suggestion with another discussion as to why the choice was not a good one. This went on for some time, hours actually and by now I was getting hungry myself and I was also behind in my stone wall building chores, another story altogether which is contained in this book. I suggested that we have some breakfast and again Grandpa rejected that idea. The rejection was for a very good reason, he had forgotten to get the necessary provisions the day before, we would have to go to the store. This was good he said, for it would allow us to get exactly what it was that we intended to put in the soup, once we fine-tuned our list of ingredients. We sat there for another half-hour or so strategizing over our plans for the soup.

He then said that there would also have to be a plan of attack for cooking this soup. What would go in, and of course, in what order. He further explained in great detail the fact that a good cook had to have intimate knowledge of the cooking times of different ingredients. He explained that this was never more important than when making good soup, especially good beef soup. You should always end up with soup that has all of the ingredients cooked to the same degree and desired consistency in order for all who partake in its ingestion to fully enjoy the soup. The size of the ingredients also was an issue in that he said that it was important for all items to be of roughly the same size as to be able to conveniently fit onto the spoon. All very good advice for sure yet, to a hungry teenage boy, a message lost, another well-intended sermon gone astray!

List in hand, we finally got into the Jeep and headed off to the store. Once there Grandpa was in fine form and went about his smelling, poking, prodding and squeezing as he carefully navigated the list of chosen ingredients. Few items were allowed to be picked that were not on the list with the exception of a few bottles of Old Grand Dad for 'snake bites' of course! Before I knew it we were on our way back to the Lodge with a bunch of bags and bottles crinkling and clanging in the back of the trusty old Jeep CJ. In short order we were back at the Lodge unloading the groceries. It was mid-morning by now and I needed some food.

Grandpa said that he would make me a sandwich, but that I should not eat much as the soup would be plenty nourishing later on, we were also going to make enough soup for a few days. He relented and made me a baloney sandwich that I quickly ate. Grandpa then suggested we sit down and get into our plan. We set about cleaning and dicing the meat that was to be the main ingredient in our feast. Next came the vegetables which had to be carefully cleaned, peeled, and then diced into like, bite-sized cubes. There were two sets of some of the veggies, one for the stock making process and then another to be injected into the actual soup. These all had to be kept separate for each had to be introduced into the broth at a specific time in the process. And there were also the seasoning agents which had to be measured for the amount of ingredients.

Gramps, I think after seeing the reflection of the mark on his forehead from the morning's baptism by mettle, had decided to use the biggest cooking pot that we had, a large copper covered cauldron of at least 10 quarts! He then said that the best method of cooking such a large kettle would in fact be in the large fireplace in the living room. To my amazement he soon discounted that idea because of the difficulties of moving fifty pounds of boiling liquid safely in the confines of the rooms connecting the living room and the kitchen area.

Only slightly better was his second choice of the grill area atop the gas range in the kitchen. This was a questionable choice as well because of the fact that neither of us could safely see over the top and into the cauldron while it was perched atop the grill. The grill it was, however, and we put the cauldron on the grill and proceeded to measure the required water with the accuracy normally afforded only precious science projects. I really do not remember the exact amount of water but it was an unbelievable amount, for soup, for just the two of us! He turned on the gas and with a strike of a match, the collected gas blast into action under the pot with a resounding whhhooomp! He said that it was necessary to wait until the water was tepid to put in the bones, carrots, and celery for the initial stock. This took a while, so I proceeded about my wall building chores. Gramps said that he would come out and get me at each and every step of the process so that I would not miss out on the excitement of soup building. In the meantime he was sipping on the occasional beer and chasers of Old Grand Dad, he was indeed the perfect foreman.

He came and got me for the initial introduction of the bones and veggies, and then again to remove them, before the rest of the soup making process could move forward. The removal of boiling hot bones and soft vegetables from a pot that you cannot see into is a rather tricky and somewhat dangerous intimidating process. It gets even more interesting if the chef, the actual 'man in charge' of the kitchen is sipping away at the hootch. Somehow, I suspect through divine intervention, we managed to get the bones and veggies out of the cauldron with no serious problems or, more importantly, grave injuries. It was now mid-afternoon and Gramps continued his vigilance and, as promised, continued to summon me at each important step of the process. Like some Biblical miracle the water was finally being transformed from a dream into mighty fine smelling soup reality. The savory smell sort of wafted around the Lodge, escaping through the doors and windows that now were wide open in an attempt to cool down the inside of the place. The entire Lodge had been heated up to an unbelievable level, as a result of the heat pouring off of this boiling cauldron. I was lucky, at least I was outside in the coolness of the late afternoon. Grandpa, however, was inside sipping away and getting not completely snapped, but certainly happy from the many visits with his Old Grand Dad.

The work of building the wall, coupled with a lack of food for the day, was giving me an extra special hunger. The whiffs of soup only made matters worse. It would not be long, however, until we could sit down and feast on this glorious creation of ours.

It was now after five and I wondered how much longer it would be. I went up into the kitchen and asked Gramps what the ETS (estimated time for soup) was and to my delight, he said that we were almost there, it was truly about time as I was near the point of starvation.

I was back outside toiling at the wall when Grandpa wobbled up and asked me to join him at the soup cauldron. He said that we were about to take the most important step in good soup making,

that being to actually 'sample' it and 'adjust' the seasoning if needed. He first took the ladle then surprisingly slowly and carefully stepped up on the stool, and slowly dipped the end over the edge of the pot, gently swirling it around. He then took it out of the pot and waited until it had cooled sufficiently so as not to singe his lips. He then raised it carefully to his mouth and sipped it like a fine wine from the ladle. He stood there savoring this concoction for a moment without saying a thing. He then slowly almost mubbling said,
"it needs something, what it needs I don't really know but there is definitely something missing". He then stepped down from the stool, handed the ladle to me and said,
"what do you think?"
I stepped up on the stool and, mimicking him slipped the ladle into the pot, stirred, and brought out an adequate amount for tasting, I gently blew on it to cool it and sipped it up.
"It tastes awesome," I said "let's eat."
Grandpa just stood there for a second and again precariously stepped up on the stool, slipped the ladle into the steamy cauldron to retrieve some soup, sipped it and said,
"I know what it needs, it needs salt. With just a little more salt, not much, this soup will be absolutely perfect."
He then got down from the stool and went over to the cabinet where he reached in and pulled out the big round Mortons salt containers so popular in the day. I remember, it was a dark blue, with a screw-on tin lid, the can had a picture of a girl with an umbrella, and she was wearing a yellow slicker. "When it rains it pours" was written prominently on the can. 'When it rains it pours", no truer words were ever spoken especially when in the control of Grandpa!

Grandpa now took the salt container and walked back over to the stool, even more gingerly got up on it, and said that this would take care of it. He pulled back the little pouring spout on the lid and put the container up and over the top of the pot. The next sound that I heard was the distinct sound of tin hitting mettle. This sound was closely followed by a series of Pirate-like expletives from Gramps. He then lifted the container up and, even to my untrained eyes, the problem became very apparent. The whole lid had come off of the container, and a huge amount of salt had found its way into the soup.

"How do you like that" he said, "somebody didn't tighten the God-damned lid on this salt container. Well, now we certainly have a problem, this soup is inedible".

He got down from the stool, turned to me and asked for suggestions on how to best remedy this rather unsavory situation. I really had none, so he suggested a few.

"We could add a lot more water, diluting the salt," he said but continued "if we do that then we will also dilute the beefy flavor as well and render the soup, at the very best, bad soup." He went on saying "We could just add more ingredients to match the added water but that would result in far too much soup, requiring more pots and utensils."

He was meandering around, thinking, I guess. He then took another swig of Old Grand Dad.

"We do not even have any more of the required extra ingredients! Even if we did after a few hours of cooking the new ingredients would be nice and tender while the original ingredients would be reduced to mush.... bad soup is the only thing we will get and we don't want bad soup, we want good soup!"

He sauntered over to the window and gazed out. He then turned in a somewhat theatrical way and looked directly into my rather hungry eyes.

"I have the solution" he proudly stated "the only really acceptable solution." He continued "Go and open the back door and find something that will keep it open."

I began having that problematic 'Grandpa' feeling in my gut, however, I did exactly what he asked. I returned to the kitchen where he, shot-glass in hand, told me to get another stool and a couple of dishcloths then to come join him at the grill. I did that as well. He then said to carefully climb the stool and, along with and in absolute harmony with him, lift this big boiling cauldron from the grill, step down from the stool and follow him, as though I had a choice!

We very carefully successfully removed the hot pot from the heat, stepped off of the stools and at almost a snail's pace made our way to, then through the back door and out onto the driveway. He said just do as he was doing and that this whole problem would be solved.

What the hell did I know, I was just a starving young teenager, so, I did what he suggested. We carefully continued with this boiling hot cauldron a couple of hundred feet up the hill behind the Lodge where there was a bit of a valley that sloped in the opposite direction, away from the place. He finally stopped and said, "This will do just fine," he continued in a very proud and confident voice "this is what you do with bad soup.... you ditch it!"
With that, he unceremoniously pushed the cauldron over, the beefy contents, albeit uber salty, poured out and slowly made it way down into the ground of the little valley below!

I stood there in amazement suffering a combination of disbelief and hunger-induced panic.
"Grab your side and help me get this God-damned thing back into the kitchen."
We made it back into the kitchen where he then had another shot of hooch and prepared another baloney sandwich for me!

We chatted for a while, then retired for the night, after all, tomorrow was yet another adventure with Grandpa just waiting to happen.

It took me far too long to figure out that Grandpa was not at all trying to teach me how to make soup that day, nor was he trying to waste our time and gastronomic resources. No, what Grandpa was trying to teach me was something extremely important about life. What Gramps was teaching me was that if something in your plan for life goes wrong, never mind trying to fix it, just pitch it and start over, it's easier, it's cheaper, and in the long run, it's cleaner. Don't waste your time, energy, and mental or emotional resources.

It was too bad that Grandpa didn't take a more direct approach in this teaching, it would have saved me much pain and misery in my adult years. In any case, over time, I learned the lesson well. The 'pot of soup' theory, if it's bad, just throw it away and simply start over again.

That is what Gramps was doing that particular day, he was teaching me that simple but invaluable 'pot of soup' lesson in life!

CHAPTER 11 – GRAMP'S WEIRD SCHOOL OF HARD KNOCKS - THE WAY TO TREAT AN ANGRY BEAR!

The forests and streams of the Adirondak Mountains in upstate New York are definitely a most challenging place to be during blackfly and No-Seeum season. Anyone who has been unfortunate enough as to encounter these creatures will know immediately of which I write. For those who do not know, however, *No-Seeum* is the name of a teensy-tiny little bug with a huge appetite and teeth like 'Jaws'. The name No-Seeum is actually a shortened version of the Indian name for these voracious little devils with the ravenous taste for animal flesh, the real name given to these creatures by the Indians was No-Seeum-Big-Bitem!

The Lodge, as we would refer to Dad's place, was built in the midst of the Adirondak Forest making it virtually impossible to escape these pests. One could always stay inside, but even this would only offer a person partial relief from the blackflies and No-Seeums during the day. At night, however, all bets were off as the lights of the non-air conditioned house and the alluring scent of the bug-held captives attracted these creatures and screens did little more than slow down and annoy the No-Seeums on their way through to indulge themselves in their nightly feast.

Humans were not the only things that found a high degree of annoyance in dealing with these bugs. Deer, Bear, Raccoons, Rabbits, in fact all creatures living were fair and open targets, there was no real escape. The best you could hope for was some form of temporary relief in the water or in some opening away from the woods. Animals are pretty smart at times, and many have figured this out also. All that an animal has to do is to get out of the woods into some clearing and as long as the creature can stay there, it will enjoy some modest relief from these blood-sucking pests.

Life itself is normally full of surprises and, as is often the case, things don't always go as planned. Life with my paternal grandfather was especially prone to surprises. One thing was certain and that was that if Grampa was around, things were going to be interesting. I was still in my pre-teenage years and was spending time, or should I say doing time, at the Lodge with

Grampa. It was nearing the end of a late spring afternoon, the sun was getting lower and the shadows were getting longer. Another day would soon be history. We had been working, sorry, I had been working, with Gramps in his supervisory state of mind. He, as was customary, was making sure that what had to be done would get done in the most disruptive manner possible and at the very last minute. In any case the work was getting done and dinner was close to becoming priority one. Grampa's supervisory role allowed him more than sufficient time to fabricate specific plans for dinner as well as giving him the essential time to organize his thoughts on what would be needed to prepare the nightly spread. The only store that was even close was Westcott's, a very typical country store out in the middle of nowhere. We would get our foodstuff and fuel for the tractor and other mechanical implements there. Westcott's was about ten miles from the Lodge and usually remained open until six or so in the evening in summertime but, you could never be sure.

We would have to go there every other day or so to get whatever perishable goods we needed to survive. Grampa would slip in a few bottles of Old Gran Dad just to be on the safe side "for snake bites" but bread, milk, eggs, and meat were usually the norm. This particular day was amongst those where we needed some things from the store so we got cleaned up a bit and headed out to the Jeep for the trek to civilization 'down the road'. Remember that this was back in the early sixties and the Lodge was out in the 'boonies'. Dad had a rule that there was always to be a loaded revolver in the Jeep. This rule resulted from the wilderness setting of the Lodge and the inherent dangers of intermingling with wild beasts. Wolves, Bears, Mountain Lions, and a host of poisonous reptiles and rodents can be very dangerous to your health especially if confronted when with their young, or if hungry, or if they are in some form of agitated state. There were few things, if any, that could drive these wild beasts crazy 'over the edge' and into a full-fledged fit of rage but No-Seeums and blackflies seemed to have graduated from Ogre Making 101 with flying colors and could do it in a flash.

We hurried to the Jeep, fired it up and were on our way. Duane Stage Road wound lazily through the woods of the valley and thus provided the only opening in the forest for miles. Traffic was not even in the vocabulary at the Lodge. There were so few cars in a normal day that when traveling this road you wouldn't even expect to encounter another car. The animals also would be oblivious to the possibility of traffic so you would always be on alert for unsuspecting beasts wandering across the road. A Jeep may be a rough, tough vehicle but it can be rendered very unstable and very unsafe if in contact with any large animal. Another consideration was the lack of protection afforded by the rather 'flimsy' metal roof and tinny doors of our Jeep. The metal top and doors were absolutely essential in the winter when operating the Jeep in temperatures that would easily render any 'brass monkey' lighter through the relief of any appendages that he may have had before being dragged off to suffer winter in the mountains around Malone.

Although unscientific, our personal experience seemed to indicate a direct relationship between the setting of the sun and the preponderance of the bloodletting insects. It was around 'that' time, that referring to the time at which these insects would begin to amass in great numbers. We had progressed about a mile and a half or so when we rounded a bend in the road to be confronted by a somewhat agitated looking black bear. The beast had figured out that if he wished to maximize his ability to evade these biting, annoying insects, his best bet was in the cleared path that we called the road. He was truly in a state of hyperactivity and somewhat comical looking movements. I thought that we would stop, or back up, or simply attempt to go around the bear, for a few seconds I had forgotten that it was Grampa who was controlling our immediate destiny.

Gramps stopped the Jeep, but just long enough to put the thing into low gear, yes the one you use if you wish to push heavy objects! A second later we were on a slow path directly towards the bear. Grampa was telling me not to worry, that he had everything under control! To illustrate what a little fool I used to be, I actually believed him, besides we had the Smith & Wesson 357 loaded, and ready to go, between the seats if the bear got too close, or too threatening. We'd simply blow him away, besides we were in a Jeep!

Grampa edged the Jeep forward until even little Stevie Wonder could have easily identified this creature as a mean, agitated bear. He edged as close as he could in fact making full contact with this frenzied, furry, growling, spitting, clawing obstacle.

"The bear had a choice to make" exclaimed Grampa, "the same as we had made, he could either move or be moved".

The bear had obviously made his choice because he was definitely not about to voluntarily go back into the woods and closer to the biting blackflies. The bear stood there even more determined and upright than before. He began to push on the front of the Jeep in an effort to hold his ground. Grampa was mumbling something about what a great advertisement this would make for Jeeps and that this was in fact where their true value lay. I was checking between the seats to make sure that the gun was still there and that it was in fact ready to go. Grampa played with the clutch and the throttle trying to get the bear off-balance but that was not going as planned. The bear, in fact, had actually pushed the Jeep a bit off track and had made another tactical move that was even more unnerving to me. He had started to move towards the edge of the hood. The bear was not only smart enough to have figured out the insect evading thing but, in scant seconds, he was discovering the rather serious sideways instability of a Jeep. He began rocking the Jeep as he slowly edged towards the driver's door area, all the time his eyes were studying the combined looks of sheer unadulterated joy and absolute terror from the two occupants. I took the gun out of the holster and told Grampa that it was ready.

"For what?" he said!

"To shoot the damned bear!" I answered.

He said that it wasn't time and that he was still in total control. I kept wondering why with the bear now not directly in our way he just didn't step on the gas and get the hell out of there. He had another plan I suspect, another questionable lesson in life just for me.

It is important to remember that the top on the Jeep was not very sturdy and was actually held on only by a couple dozen small sheet metal screws. The bear was now directly by the driver's door and had stretched his paws to the edge of the top. He had figured out that leverage was an advantage to him in that he could shake the stupid Jeep even more violently if he pushed on the top. Not only that, but the anchor screws were making all sorts of frightening noises as they began to work loose.

Mesmerized by the blatant disregard for safety by the two 'willing' participants, the third 'unwilling' party, me, could do little but sit idly by as Grampa blurted out that he finally had the bear right where he wanted him! "Watch this" Grampa proudly said, "this is how you handle a bear"!

I held the gun in my shaking hand as much to my horror Grampa began slowly rolling down the damned window! The bear was still highly involved in 'Jeep tossing' and did not really seem too surprised at the window going down. The opening window allowed the black flies to invade the interior of the Jeep. Accompanying these bugs was an unpleasant assortment of distasteful odors and sounds emanating from the bear. Still, Grampa continued carefully lowering the window until there was just enough space for the bear to stick his snout in.

My great lesson in life was about to come to an end within the blink of an eye. Grampa, without skipping a beat, let the bear have it full force right on the nose! There was sort of a 'schmack' sound that resulted from this sucker punch. It definitely was one of the greatest right hooks that I have ever witnessed, Sonny Liston would have been proud. The bear reeled back in absolute surprise, amazement, and I'm sure some nasal discomfort.

That poor unsuspecting beast, like many, many other creatures, had paid the price of attempting to outmaneuver Grampa. He could only watch as Grampa hit the gas, swatting at the blackflies in the Jeep and bellowing as we hurtled away and disappeared off into the distance.

Grampa was right again, he did have everything under control and even more unbelievable was that we were actually still alive, and there was not even one shot fired!

Thank the good Lord, stupidity is not always a self-correcting problem!

CHAPTER 12 – NO TICKY, NO LAUNDRY!
(JESUIT JUSTICE AT ITS FINEST)

As I grew older, not necessarily more mature, the lessons in real life came at an increasing rate and were far more direct, presenting themselves with little or no camouflage to soften the blow. One of, if not the most important lessons in life was tastefully administered to me personally at the hands of the all-loving, all-caring, all-giving Holy Catholic Order of the Jesuit priests.

I had been a 'ward' of the Jesuits for some four years resulting from me being 'sentenced' by my parents to Regiopolis College, the name meaning the King's College. 'Regi' was a 'boarding' high school run by the ultra-strict order of the Jesuits. I, as did most of my captive classmates, found Regiopolis more prison-like than other high-brow institutions of learning. One thing that was a factor in that way of thinking was that Kingston was well recognized as the home to three Federal Penitentiaries, all with electric chairs that were being put to good use on a regular basis back then and all of these 'Pen' buildings looking suspiciously just like Regi! It was not all that uncommon for us to be in class or in the study room when all of the lights would flicker and dim, a sign that some poor inmate was having their personal lights turned off permanently. The priests who could see that we all knew what was going on would, in a very caring and psychologically soothing way, tell us not to worry, it was just some miscreant being 'fried in the chair' for a life not reflecting their or God's views. They would lecture us on just how bad these Federal prisoners were, killers, rapists, just the absolute dregs of society.

And wouldn't you know it, for all of the 'Formals' held at the school it they would actually bring in bands from these prisons, the very people that they lectured us about constantly, warning us that only evil could result from any and all contact with these 'scum of the earth'. We would be out there 'dancing the night fantastic' with one eye on our dates and the other eye making sure that none of the members of the band broke free from the chains anchoring them to the legs of the piano!

I actually liked learning and was a very good student with well above-average grades. As a matter of fact while in Grade 10 I was also attending some classes at Queens University, another prestigious learning institution in Kingston in preparation for college hopefully to get a degree in medicine. Well as most of us have learned what you want and what you get is more often than not something totally different. Such was my case.

Things were not going well for my mother at home, as I toiled away at school I would often get calls from Mom, crying and venting about the terrible situation that Dad had created for her, actually all of us, at home. She had little or no money thus little or no food and the landlord was at the end of his 'wits' and was threatening to throw her out of the house, something that ultimately did happen. In one call she asked if she could sell my prized possession, a 54 Chevy, so that she could buy groceries. How could I possibly say no? I was just in my early teens and already very psychologically conflicted.

The school year was almost over so I figured that I could hang in until after 'finals' then get home and see what I could do to help. Final exams came and went and I knew that I had aced most of them so all that was left was to wait a few more days for graduation ceremonies at which point I would have my diploma in hand and be homeward bound.

I remember being down in the recreational room at 'Regi' playing pool with a couple of friends when one of the priests approached me and said that the Principal wished to see me in his office, a strange command especially in the evening. A multitude of thoughts went through my mind, most of them concerning Mom and the possibility of some disastrous news about her. Well the 'news' was indeed disastrous but it had nothing to do with Mom.

The Principal, a stern (*redundant* word!) Jesuit priest that we respectfully referred to as the 'warden', invited me into the office and sat me down for a 'talk'. He went through a litany of things that I had accomplished in my time at Regiolpolis and how the future held nothing but tremendous promise for me. He then read out loud the results of my final exams which confirmed exactly what I had thought, I had in fact 'aced' them all in reality getting a

99% in Physics, the highest score ever at that institution. I was of course elated, however, the elation was very short-lived.
"We have a huge problem." he then said.
"Your bill for the last two semesters has not been paid and unless it is paid before graduation we cannot give you anything, no transcripts of your test results and definitely not your graduating diploma!"
I was flattened.
"Get a hold of your father and get the bill paid and all of this will be forgiven."

I left in a state of panic. I got on the phone, a pay phone by-the-way in the hallway at the school and tried for hours to track down Dad, all was in vain.

The next day I plead for my scholastic life with the Principal and anyone else who would listen, again an exercise in futility.

God indeed works in mysterious ways even through his most holy, most loving, most giving personal representatives on earth. Graduation at Regiopolis came and went that year and I never, not to this day, ever got my grades or my graduation diploma.

The most holy Fathers steadfastly refused to budge an inch stating that it would set a bad example if they were to let me slide through without getting their just rewards!

That very evening I borrowed the necessary money from some of my better-off buddies and was on a train homeward bound with absolutely nothing to show for my years at Regi other than my own memories and one positive long-term thing, a great lesson in life that would in fact serve me well long into the future.

CHAPTER 13 – I Can Fly, I Can Fly!

Not all stories in this book are funny, some are in fact very serious, however, almost all are somewhat disturbing in many ways, this is definitely one of the latter.

I was eight or nine years of age, old enough that I really should have known better. We had just finished dinner and I had announced that I was going to take my bicycle and go see a friend. It was on one of those infrequent evenings when Dad was actually home, fortunately or unfortunately, I just haven't figured that part out yet.

Just before I went out the door Dad hollered to me,
"Make sure that you look both ways before you go out of the driveway."
He obviously was all too familiar with my dare devilish 'Banzai' bicycle riding style.
"OK" I hollered back and out the door to the garage I went to get the bike. I got on and quickly sped out of the driveway as fast as my little legs could peddle and directly on to Senneville Road. Just as I remembered Dad's warning I heard the unmistakable sounds of tires screeching, I looked and before I could react I saw the front end of a black 1950 Ford barreling down on me!

There was little I could do and the car, unable to stop hit me. To make matters worse, if that were possible, the '50 Ford cars had a rather large and very pointed chrome 'bullet' in the center of the grill. In any case the last that I remembered before going 'airborne' was that awesomely designed shiny bullet hitting my left side, I could hear all sorts of cracking going on inside of me. The force of the impact resulted in being flung into the air with me actually flying over the stone wall that surrounded the house. I came to rest against the side of the garage, for all of you air travel aficionados out there, a flight of some twenty feet or so, actually not bad for a beginner! The car ran over my bike demolishing it in the process, yet another bike hit the dust in Senneville.

The driver got out of the car in a state of absolute panic and somehow scrambled over the wall to my rescue, he was very, very relieved and somewhat amazed that, not only was I alive but I was seemingly in pretty good shape with minimal bleeding and no apparent broken bones. I shared this man's amazement in that during the short garage-bound flight I thought I was going to die, my short but eventful life flashing before my little eyes.

Other than getting my 'bell rung' and a few aches and pains, I felt pretty good. The driver helped me to stand up and walk around a bit then said that he would get his car and my mangled bike and take me up to the house. I begged and pleaded with him not to take me to the house but he was insistent that he talk to someone about what had happened. My reluctance was based in my inner fear of facing Dad after his warning not to do exactly what I ended up doing!

Before I knew it we were at the front door of the house with the man explaining to Dad and Mom how he could not possibly have avoided me as I just came out of the driveway without stopping or without even looking, oh crap I thought to myself. After a few more minutes of chatting and exchanging names and phone numbers the man left and I was there facing an obviously irritated Dad.

Without saying a word and with little or no resistance from Mom, Dad grabbed me by the scruff of the neck and pulled me up the stairs to my room where he then picked me up and actually threw me across the room, lucky for me I landed on the bed. Again in retrospect I suspect that Dad's throwing ability was better than I thought and that he intended for me to land exactly where I did on a soft target. In any case I was airborne, on my own for the second time in an hour or so, just how lucky can one young lad get?

Very seldom does one get away from almost certain disaster without paying some price. A day or so later I fell about two feet out of a tree and broke my left collarbone, go figure. In retrospect I believe that I actually cracked it when I got hit by the car and it subsequently snapped when I fell.

Dad was really not a careless or heartless person deep down inside, he often acted like he was but it was not his real nature to be mean or cruel. Regardless, without checking for injuries such as broken bones, throwing a young kid who had just been hit by a car across a room seems to me to fit into the careless or heartless category.

The somewhat strange thing about this episode, at least to me to this very day, is that it is not being hit by the car that sticks in my mind, it was the absolutely carefree way that Dad tossed me across my room. Again, maybe I am making too much of this, maybe that's just the way they used to do things back then when you were from Cincinnati!

CHAPTER 14 – Energy Conservation, Grandpa Style!

The wind howled and the storm continued its lashing of the Lodge in the typical Upstate New York blizzard. I knew that it was Saturday morning but you wouldn't have known it by looking outside, the sun was nowhere to be seen. It was dark, cold and just plain miserable. Dad used to brag about the fact that the Lodge was a mere twelve miles from Owls Head, NY, the coldest spot in the Northeast! He wasn't joking for there were a couple of nights each year on average where the thermometer would plunge to below fifty below zero without the wind chill factored in! I recall one night where it was forty-eight below zero. My brother George had convinced both of us that if we were to take a pot of boiling water outside and throw the water into the air, that it would be frozen solid when by the time it came back down to hit the ground. Our blisters were gone in a week or so and the throbbing soreness wasn't really that bad. Even though it was somewhat painful it turned out to be a positive in my psychological development in that I did learn a lesson in assuming that others are in fact smarter than me.

This particular day of this blizzard, however, was far more temperate with the temperature probably right around the zero mark. It was mid January after all and a good steady storm was the norm. This blizzard, however, had started some two days earlier and had dumped three feet of snow or more on top of the substantial blanket of the white stuff which already lay on the landscape. The wind was whipping and swirling this snow into white mini-tornados and then dropping it forming tremendous drifts. Beautiful stuff indeed, if you like blizzards.

The Lodge itself lay in a small valley which snaked along between two medium sized mountains. The structure itself was built into the foothills of the mountain to the rear. The garage and parking area were in a cleared-out tract out front of the house which seemed to be the exact spot where Mother Nature liked unloading all the snow that She had gathered from the surrounding areas. This spot, unfortunately, was also the exact location of choice for Grampa to park his beloved car. There was a large garage in which there was plenty of room for his car, but the great outdoors seemed to be more to his liking, and the great outdoors was were the car was left to battle the hostile elements.

There was a combination of coincidental happenings going on that were to shape our activities for that day. The blizzard, although always anticipated, had somehow seemingly caught Grampa by surprise. As far as me and my brother went, we were sort of innocent by-standers in this. It wasn't as though we didn't have fair warning but in retrospect, I think that our ability to retain our functionality as a group was somewhat hindered by Grampa's earlier normal ingestion of what he referred to as his antifreeze, a store bought remedy for what 'ails you' appropriately named Old Grandad.

The fact that we got caught off guard only became important because Fridays were normally the time to stock up on the necessary provisions for the coming week and we had already been low on some of the essentials. At the same time as we were pondering our fate, the unmistakable sounds of the snowplow could be heard. This in itself was strange because of the remote location of the Lodge and the road upon which it was located being such an infrequently traveled one, plowing was usually done only well after the end of any storm. We had a Jeep for emergencies complete with tire chains and a plow. It, by the way, was in fact parked in the warmth and safety of the garage along with the tractor, so we were not really ever stranded.

Well, we were hungry, the dog wanted to go out, Grampa wanted to start his car, and the plow had miraculously cleared the road. In a fit of near natural behavior Gramps decided it might be a good time to drive to the store for our weekly provisions. It was a trek of some ten miles each way. We got all bundled up and made our way down towards the car. You could make out where the car was but it was embedded in a huge snow drift that went from the roof of the nearby tool shed down over the car's roof sloping from the windshield to the front of the hood. The plow had also deposited a rather large amount of snow directly in front of the car so it was certainly not in the best situation for its use in our quest for food, soon to be our great adventure du jour, thanks to Gramps. I thought that intelligence and circumstances would have dictated that the Jeep would have been a better choice of vehicle for this trek, however Grampa's undeniable wisdom and wealth of experience won out and the '54 Ford was the chosen vehicle.

In preparation for our departure I thought that I would help by clearing the snow from the top and hood of the car. I asked Grampa where the snow brush was. You could almost hear the mental gears churning and buzzing in the old guys head. One thing that Grampa always took pride in was his self-professed ability to teach others, especially younger soon to be victims of his teachings, how to handle the real necessities in life. Here was another opportunity for him to shine and I guess I was responsible for the upcoming lesson. After I asked for the snow brush, which I considered to be a somewhat obvious question, he simply answered "why"!

Grandpa was an equal opportunity psychological destabilization machine and you could almost hear this wonderfully-frightening machine firing up in the old guy's brain. He gathered George and I to his side and began to tell us that people should try to save their energy whenever possible, especially in stormy weather where at any given moment something could happen that would necessitate a person to muster up all of the energy possible to perform tasks just to stay alive. He continued and said that the situation that we faced was a great example of an opportunity for someone to expend almost no energy yet get the job done. He then told me to go get a broom. I trudged back up to the Lodge a fetched a broom then lumbered back down to the parking lot and gave Gramps the broom.

He then slowly walked around to the front of the car and stood there, almost transfixed for a moment, then holding the broom by the straw end crouched down a bit and said aloud "this should be just about right" then in a smooth fluid movement slowly poked two holes into the snow on the hood which went from the front straight through to the windshield. He sort of twisted the broom around in order to enlarge the holes. These holes were about eye level and were separated by a space about the width of Grampa's nose. We were definitely in for a lesson in life, however, I have always been one that enjoyed the more exciting dangerous side of things so Grampa's lesson seldom let me down.

Grampa then told us to get in the car, relax and just watch what would happen. He then got in, slowly closed the door, got comfortable, started the car and in countdown like fashion, prepared for takeoff, squinting and focusing as best he could through his tunnel-like apertures, now we were seeing the real Grandpa emerge!.

He put the Ford in first gear and slowly let the clutch out, the car started creeping forward and slipping and sliding actually sort of begrudgingly plowed through the snow bank left by the plow, wow we were on the road and ready to go.
"Hang on guys, this is how you clear snow off of your car."
He shifted into second gear and was squinting through the holes trying to see where we were going with the intensity of a heart surgeon trying to see through blood. The car skidded a bit as he hit the gas. Gramps successfully maneuvered the car around the first corner after which there was a bit of a straight stretch of road.
"Here we go guys, watch this."
We simply sat there, unable to see a thing but being fully aware that the car in which we rode was picking up speed. We also knew that there was a series of bends in the road that were fast approaching, missing any of them would certainly result in the car going over the edge most likely into the frozen river below.

Much to our dismay Gramps just stayed on the gas, with little warning and nothing but a dull thud all of a sudden the entire collection of snow that obscured our vision and covered the hood of that old Ford was gone, it blew off from the gathering speed of the car.

"That's better" is all that Gramps said as he flopped back into the driver's seat and turned the windshield wipers on. Even though the roads still remained extremely dangerous, especially when someone like Gramps was at the wheel, I was somewhat comforted, at least I could see what was about to happen.

Again, when it came to Grandpa and his questionable Old Grand Dad induced antics I am glad that stupidity is not always a self-correcting problem!

Looking Back on a Warped but Wonderful Childhood

CHAPTER 15 – Dad, Duchess and Customs Officers

One of, if not the only time that I ever saw Dad physically cry, was one truly dreadful afternoon, the afternoon that we had to take Duchess, our truly awesome Great Dane on her last 'ride' to put her down. She was my first dog, not just a dog but my trusted friend and I was absolutely shattered to the point of being near suicidal, hell, I still am brought to tears when I think about it and its some sixty years later! Dad was crying because he also evidently loved that dog, we all did. His obvious love for Duchess, however, was not always evident, as least to me and my developing brain.

Dad, from time to time in reality but, in my mind far too frequently, would don a trench coat, put on one of his full-face masks, a police-type hat and boxing gloves then go around the back of the house where Duchess was kept on a chain, a long chain but a chain none-the-less. Dad would then, without saying a word, proceed to physically harass and taunt poor Duchess into a rage where he would carefully place himself at the very end of Duchess's reach. He would then begin a systematic hitting of her with his fists and of all things, the 'police' hat. I would watch in a somewhat conflicted and confused state, often trying to intervene on poor Duchess's behalf but always to no avail. This activity would last 10 minutes or so and through it all Dad would not say a word. He would simply go back around the house and disappear. I would attempt to comfort Duchess who must have been even more confused as I was.

Many, many times I would confront Dad about his obvious physical abuse of Duchess, his response was always that I should wait until all of the facts and motives were in! For better or for worse that time was about to take place.

Dad was an International business man who was not above bribery, particularly on the Canadian side of the border. He had actually gained a bit of notoriety as a result of his ethically-challenged business and law-enforcement targeted motivated philanthropy. He was a master at it, realizing that if he 'specialized' in items that were either absolutely cost-prohibitive or, better yet totally unavailable in Canada, the numbers of 'blind eyes' that could be bought could be optimized. To do so required creativity and creativity was yet another exceptionally important piece in Dad's personal people motivating arsenal.

He was also not above, let me find the proper words here, uh, smuggling! In fact smuggling of goods into Canada was an integral part in his way of doing business. Dad had the Lodge, a wonderful getaway nestled in the Adirondack Mountains outside of Malone in the 'real' upstate of New York in the United States. The Lodge was about 90 miles or so from our house in Senneville, a village in Quebec which of course is in Canada.

Dad was doing business, supposedly selling locomotives, in almost all areas of the world. On his return from his many global jaunts, he would bring all sorts of stuff back from England, Europe, Asia and Mexico, items that were either too expensive to buy in the US and Canada or, as stated earlier totally unavailable elsewhere. He would then stash these items at the Lodge in his 'office'. The office was a fortified bunker-like room with a near-impenetrable steel-clad door with and windows high up on the wall far too small for all but the tiniest of adults to even attempt to crawl through, definitely a Dad design to discourage anyone from seeing anything in that room, that is unless he wanted you to.

Exotic foreign cheeses, Jade and sculptures from India and Turkey, Cameras from Germany and Japan, the list of 'ferried' items went on and on, all secreted away in the office at the Lodge. This awesome collection would be 'doled out' at Dad's discretion to those who could either 'look the other way' or change rules, regulations or laws to accommodate Dad's business wishes. The main impediment in this plan was that in most cases these items had to be brought into Canada and in Dad's case, without the Canadian Customs officials and law enforcement agencies at large knowing it. as I stated, Dad was not lacking in creativity.

In order to go to the Lodge from home, or the other way, you had to go through an official border-crossing station, in this case located at Trout River, NY. It was also an immigration post so it was always well-staffed with very official looking officers in very official looking uniforms, including of course, police-type hats.

One afternoon Dad came home and asked if I wanted to go to the Lodge with him, he said that we would take Duchess along for the ride, to do so would require that we take Mom's Chevy station wagon. I of course was ready to go even before I answered. Just to add a few details to the story, the Chevy station wagon had a rear facing passenger seat that when folded down was covered with a thick rubber mat, unless you knew that it was there it was truly inconspicuous. The cushions on the seats were also removable making the 'hidden' space under the floor far more voluminous than with them in place, the perfect space to transport Dad's illegal hidden treasures from the Lodge.

I knew right away when Dad started removing the cushions from the Chevy that we were going to be in for an interesting ride as well as an even more interesting one of Dad's lessons in life. He quickly placed the seat cushions in the garage and then went and got Duchess and loaded her into the rear of the station wagon. Without further ado we were off.

The ride was great with Duchess taking in the scenery and seemingly totally enjoying her travels. An hour or so had passed and we were fast approaching the border crossing at Trout River.
"Don't say a word when we get to customs," Dad said "you will see why I sometimes treat Duchess the way I do. You will love it!"

We got to the border and pulled up to the Customs official at which point Dad lowered his window. Dad used to go through Trout River a lot and the agents were somewhat familiar with him, the station wagon was different, he would normally have been in the Corvette or Caddy convertible. The Custom agent struck up a conversation with Dad and went through the normal prerequisite questions. Without even being asked Dad got out and walked around the back of the car, I could hear Duchess let out a muffled but unmistakable deep growl. I could also hear Dad as he asked the agent if he wanted to check the inside of the back of the car. Dad slowly opened the rear flip up window of the car upon which the agent started leaning forward with his official hat-ladened head in an effort to see inside... Duchess went nuts! She was showing her teeth, growling and spitting and doing her utmost to get at the agent who quickly stepped away from the car demanding that Dad close the window to contain the dog. Dad of course did so and apologized profusely to him. The agent, thankful to be alive sent us on our way through the border into the US and back on our way to the Lodge.

Dad as was his normal routine stopped at the next gas station which was owned and operated by some nearly blind old guy amply named Blinky, he was downright dangerous with his windshield cleaning spray bottle, especially if you were in a convertible. Dad got out, opened the rear window and gave Duchess a big hug. He then got back in.
"What did you think of that?" Dad said to me with a huge smile on his face, "that's how you handle customs agents. You will see, Duchess will be even better on the way home."
We got gassed up, Dad paid Blinky and we were once again on the road. We soon arrived at the Lodge where we would spend another great weekend.

Monday morning rolled around and after breakfast Dad started loading the back of the car with all sorts of 'loot' from his office. After he was done packing the car and securing the rear mat in place he loaded Duchess into the rear of the wagon and we were homebound, we did, however, have to get through customs. I was indeed just an innocent young lad but I was fully aware of the consequences of smuggling goods across the border in fact having been taught that by none other than Dad himself.

To make sure that he would impact my brain with all of the dramatic effect possible as he drove closer to the border he would remind me of the illicit cargo that we were carrying and the numerous consequences that we, yes we, would face if discovered at the border. It was working and I was actually scared to death picturing me in some isolated prison cell to waste my sorry-ass little life away in captivity.

Again we approached the border crossing at Trout River and again Dad instructed me to be quiet and just observe what was happening. Dad did exactly as he had done on the way down with exactly the same results.

Duchess went absolutely berserk in the rear of the car and the poor agent was just about crapping himself in the process of trying to escape with his life.

As we drove away from Customs Dad was reaching back to comfort and praise Duchess and with an even bigger grin on his face than a few days before he looked over at me and simply said, "Wasn't that awesome?"

Dad was indeed pretty cool sometimes, even if occasionally it was in a larcenous non-law-abiding way!

CHAPTER 16 – The Orphanage

I am inserting this story in this book on 'childhood' even though, as you will soon see, it actually took place when I was well on my way down the actual path of life. That sort of brings up the age-old question of at what exact point in one's life does childhood end, or does it ever really end? You know, it's sort of like how for up in the room does a fly soar until he turns upside down to land on the ceiling?

In any case, I was 30 years old or so and I was watching the old Johnny Carson show late one night. Johnny and Ed had progressed beyond their routine 'Schlaussen' cut-off jokes, you remember "just drive until you get to the Schlaussen cut-off, stop, then cut off your schlaussen". I digress, anyway they were doing another one of their normal segments which showed foreign television commercials, most of which were pretty funny. This one particular featured foreign ad that night showed a row of Japanese children in a common bath and there were suspicious bubbles surfacing around one of the kids, it was quite funny and kind of out of the norm at the time. What I was left with and what stuck in my mind was not the bubbles or the bath, it was that they were indeed in an orphanage. The ad hit me with a very strange sort of a 'deja vue' feeling in my brain. I watched the rest of the show and dropped off to sleep.

I awoke the next morning with that image of the boys in the orphanage still resonating in my head. Now it was more than just a feeling, it was more like an actual memory, not really clear but it was certainly there. Sometime later in the day I was talking to one of my older sisters and I mentioned the Johnny Carson episode. I asked her if she recalled me being in an orphanage when I was very young. I could tell by the tone of her voice that she thought I was having some sort of a mental problem. Her answer was a definite no, no way, no. She asked why would I have been put into an orphanage? I had to admit that it certainly was a weird, irrational thought but it was there none-the-less. Keep in mind that at that time I had four older sisters and an older brother all living at home. They certainly would have noticed my disappearance wouldn't they? Another coincidence that came to mind was that two of my

Looking Back on a Warped but Wonderful Childhood

Dad's sisters were nuns, and they had been teaching in an orphanage just across the river from Cincinnati.

Weeks went by before I got the weird feeling in my 'gut' again this time, however, I recalled not only being in the orphanage but also an incident where I somehow managed to get up onto the high diving platform where I then proceeded to fall off, obviously without dying but none-the-less very traumatic. Now that I think about it there may well have been some resultant brain damage which lingers on but then again, I suspect that any weirdness in me today is not from this episode, it is most likely simply because I am from Cincinnati.

Not being one to give up easily, I again decided to see if there could be any basis for my mind's rather strange game. This time I figured I would go right to the source so I called Mom. We did our normal thing and chatted for a while about all sorts of nonsense. Mom was great to call, she always had answers to questions that begged for more questions. It always went something like this:
"How are you doing Mom?"
"Oh, I'll be okay, I guess."
"Why, what's the matter?"
"The fireman said I'll be fine."
"What, why were the firemen there?"
"Because the police called them."

She was always full of tastefully subdued, cliff-hanger answers. After a while of chattering I got around to asking if there was any time that I was put into an orphanage. There was a resonating silence on the other end of the phone for a moment or so. "Don't be silly, why would you have been put in an orphanage?" she said. "We took you over to visit with your aunts on occasion, but stay there, never."

Well that was my answer, probably just a misguided brain wave, sort of like Jacob Marley's raw potato dilemma.

Over the next years I would offer up occasional, somewhat veiled questions to my brother and sisters regarding me being in an orphanage, these queries in almost all cases resulted in nothing more than scoffing laughter from them and amazement that I would even ask about such an asinine supposition. In all honesty I also thought that it was more than strange that I would believe deep down inside that anything like that could have occurred, after all someone in my family surely would have noticed my absence, at least that is what I would have hoped for.

My 'orphanage' folly soon morphed into a family joke, whenever our gang would get together it would always surface, but only in a comical way. I actually started thinking along the same lines... it had to be some strange mental misstep by me.

Years and years went by. My brother and sisters used to congregate a number of times each year at various houses to celebrate holidays, birthdays and the like. On this one particular occasion we had all gathered for some family event and were well into it. We were all having a great time when Mom appeared on the balcony and asked to speak with me. I was actually in the middle of doing something important, something that had to be done and could not wait, at least not for long. I went up to see Mom who was actually in earshot of some of my sisters and the kids.
"You were in the orphanage" she blurted out, her eyes tearing. Without saying another word she turned and walked back inside the house, I was at a loss for words just having my suspicions confirmed. Although I had a thousand questions starting to flow through my brain I could see Mom crying in the house and I, well I simply took the easy way out for both of us and went back to whatever it was that I was doing.

Subsequently and most unfortunately for me whenever I asked Mom anything about the 'orphanage' thing she would say nothing but that she couldn't really talk about it. To the day she died I never got any other information as to why I was in the orphanage, how long I was in the orphanage or any other detail regarding the ordeal.

God truly works in very, very mysterious ways and the only other confirmation I received regarding me being in the orphanage came at of all times, at my Mother's funeral!

In attendance at Mom's memorial service was one of my aunts who was one of the nuns at the orphanage during the time of my 'kiddy' incarceration. We were enjoying the customary meal when my aunt, the nun, walked over to me and my wife and, in a very ordinary tone said that I actually had been a guest of the orphanage for a 'while'. The setting was not conducive to any real interrogation of this frail, old 'lady of the cloth'. Even after a bit of attempting by me for her to open up she simply shut up, stood up and left without offering up any other information. She too has now passed and with her went any chance of obtaining any further information on my stay at the orphanage.

It's probably better this way in that I suspect that whatever answers would have been offered up would have resulted in nothing less than many even more unsettling questions.

Over the years I have scoured the internet and agency files where I managed to find a number of questionable bits of information regarding the Covington Orphanage and its somewhat dark post-war relationships with even darker, more appalling International organizations. Much to my dismay, like in the case of the Duplessis Orphans in Quebec, there were no solid answers contained in anything I found… just what I needed to see, a personal invitation to search further!

I suspect that I too will leave this living dimension with few if any real answers to this very seriously unnerving episode in my life.

EPILOGUE

In my mind, back when I was ten or eleven years of age and actually right up to today, Dad was one awesome guy, a total absolute failure as a father and a husband but one hell of a friend and teacher of 'all things life' especially to me as a pre-teen and teenage hell-raiser, like I said..BAD FATHER, GOOD FRIEND!

Friends, however, in the vast majority of cases are not necessarily the greatest guardians of your life. Really serious guardians should and would be constantly watching out for your well-being, regardless. This is especially true if you are attracted to the more dangerous forms of behavior as you plow through the outer-edges of life. The caveat herein is that if your so-called guardian is also prone to erratic, questionable, and highly dangerous activities, your 'guardianed' life may be 'toast' at any time, without warning.

Such was the case with me and Dad. In fact many, many friends and relatives have commented, many of them using somewhat vulgar terms, on exactly how utterly irresponsible and careless he really was involving me and his directives and guidance to me as a young lad, especially when I was at the 'Lodge'. If truth be told, and I guess this is it, now that I again look back on my adolescent years I may very well be inclined to agree.

A great example of this involved me, a quarter-mile of stone wall behind the Lodge that had to be built, old number 28 which was a rather 'baffed-out' very well-used '48 Ford stock car and, of course, Dad.

I had demonstrated a need for speed and a fiery desire to race cars and motorcycles from a very, very early age. Dad also shared that same need for speed and was sympathetic to my needs, actually becoming the first 'enabler' in my quest to experience life at high speed. This combination allowed Dad to piece together one of those deals that one could not afford to refuse, especially a young gun such as I.

Dad needed a stone retaining wall to be built along the driveway behind the Lodge. The task not only involved building the wall but the stones with which it was to be constructed had to be searched out, retrieved and transported to the site. Now Dad had a jeep and a rugged utility trailer that could be used for this job, however, I was only twelve or thirteen years of age, far too young to have a driver's license.

Dad also had a very close friend in Malone, probably closer than she should have been, a great looking thirty-some year old curvaceous female of course whose aging father was selling his treasure of a stock car. Dad figured that he could kill a few birds with one stone and concocted a deal whereby he would buy the old stocker and barter it off to me in return for me building the wall. He approached me with a 'plan' and of course, with the big yellow beast of an actual race-ready stock car dangling in front of me, I was totally and completely unable to say no. Dad further sweetened the deal by arranging to re-tag the Jeep and trailer as 'farming implements' which would legally allow me to drive them albeit with absolutely minimal legality! This move, however, allowed me to not only use the Jeep to retrieve the stones necessary for the wall but also to use the Jeep and trailer to transport the stock car to and from a local dirt track. That was the 'clincher', I caved and was about to learn more than a few ultra-valuable lessons from Dad, lessons that ultimately proved to be invaluable to me as I went through life as an adult.

It took months of back-breaking physical labor to retrieve the stones and build the wall. From early morning to sundown I could be found toiling away behind the Lodge carefully placing stone upon stone in a weird 'artsy' way to ensure that Dad would be fully satisfied with the end result. After hours and hours of laboring away at the wall I would have little energy left to work on the darn stock car. In actuality I only managed to get to the track twice all summer instead most of the 'seat' time in the car was actually spent speeding up and down the many tortuous local dirt roads like some half-crazed adolescent 'moonshiner'. The car was really an awesome race car with a rudimentary roll cage, minimal bodywork especially up front and the floor removed for weight savings and also to allow the driver to check out the front right tire while driving. The car also had a 'header' exhaust system with pipes extending just beyond the engine itself. The combination of this header type exhaust system and a floorless car allowed much of the exhaust gasses and road grime to freely invade the so-called sanctity of the driver's compartment.

I recall one weekend when my sister Carol was at the Lodge for some very, very rare get-together for some reason that I cannot even fathom at this point. I was down working on the car when she approached me asking for a ride. She was dressed in a great looking white outfit which was definitely not the proper attire for any ride in the beast, however, she was persistent suggesting that if I took it easy and didn't go crazy all would be fine. I relented and she carefully crawled in positioning herself as best she could in this sans-floor devil and hanging on to whatever she could find that was solidly mounted to the frame.

I fired the car up and dropped the clutch and off we went down dusty Duane Stage Road. I shifted into second gear and gave it some gas, the car lurched forward and then let out a loud backfire! The backfire spit out a tremendous amount of oil-filled smoke which when combined with the dirt and dust from the road created a sooty, sticky, black goo that would stick to anything and everything, including Carol and her then not-so-lovely outfit! I remember upon our return to the Lodge her extricating herself from the car and just standing there like some 'B' movie version of a transvestite Al Jolson, it was priceless.

The second and last time I actually managed to get to the race track, however, was late in the summer. The wall thank goodness was almost complete. I was about to learn a lesson, a lesson that should have been an obvious one but one that had somehow eluded me up till then. While I was in the pits one of the other so-called racers had a car similar to mine up for sale for fifty dollars, a price that I just could not accept as true but regardless of my disbelief, fifty bucks was what everyone around was saying it was really worth. I remember driving back to the Lodge that night with the fifty dollar amount in my brain being divided by the hours I had spent on the wall. It worked out to about seventeen cents an hour! I managed to take a deal to build a wall draining each and every ounce of my energy in the process for weeks on end for a return equivalent to a lousy seventeen cents for every single hour worked!

I remember bringing up what I figured was the unfairness of this deal to Dad who simply looked into my eyes and said "son, you should always be careful of all things that may tempt you, there is always, always a negative price to be paid for satisfaction".
Boy, as I was to find out later in life, he was right on!

He also explained that there were extenuating circumstances that had to be taken into the equation for instance the fact that I was too young to legally drive and the fact that without doing that deal I would have never got that race car at that time.

That was also the night he told me the joke about the guy that went to his doctor enquiring whether he had anything that could make him smarter. The doctor went into the back of his office and emerged with a small bottle of what he called 'smart' pills and prescribed two per day.

The man went home and was compliant for a day or so but could no longer stand the stench and taste of the pills so he went back to the doctor.
"Doc" he said "these pills taste like rabbit poop, I just can't take any more of them."
The doc responded with a smile, "they are rabbit poop, see, you're getting smarter already!"

That was Dad! He always had a way of making me feel a little better about everything, good or bad. As I look back on the whole stock car thing even though it was in reality a true case of indentured servitude it was also a very, very good deal for me. It offered up an unequalled opportunity to a young lad to live out a part of his life in an unbelievably satisfying crazy and dangerous way that no other so-called caring parent would have ever allowed. Life at the Lodge was physically demanding but sort of surreal, totally unlike any other place that I could think of.

Normally whatever Dad would say would happen would indeed happen, sort of like Robert DeNiro's character in the movie 'Analyze This', he had a 'gift'.

Dad consistently used to say that he was going to die at 57, well, he was wrong. He died at 58! I know that this deserves a further explanation. Dad was somewhat of an international playboy who enjoyed everything to excess. His mantra was "everything in moderation except moderation"! He would normally sleep only five nights a week and then only four or five hours on those nights. He would explain to me and others that this schedule would allow him to live as many hours awake as if he lived a 'normal' lifestyle to 90 but he would live these days and hours while he was still young enough to fully savor them, he certainly was right about that one!

He used to also routinely warn me not to expend all of my entrepreneurial energy until I reached the age of forty or so, assuming that I would actually reach forty or so. He suggested that unless you were a well-educated expert in an area of commerce requiring such expertise, few if any executives would take you seriously, you just could not have what it takes to garner the essential respect. I toiled at many positions in my formative business years with some pockets of success sporadically coming my way, however, it was only when I approached the ripe old age of forty that things took a serious turn towards consistent, steady success.

I managed to 'infiltrate' the medical community as a 'strategic medical marketing consultant' working with Siemens out of Germany on the successful systemic integration of MRI into the mainstream health care delivery system. That opened the doors to continued success for me introducing, educating the global medical communities and ultimately integrating Optimized-Pressure Lithotripsy for optimized treatment of kidney and ureteral stones and Cardiovascular CT for the detection, identification and quantification of Coronary Artery Disease even in its most challenging manifest stages.

This success has brought about many, many blessings at all levels of life and the ability to fully enjoy same. My position also allowed me access to a level of professionals, especially hyper-skilled medical specialists who otherwise would have been inaccessible to the likes of me.

Looking Back on a Warped but Wonderful Childhood

There are a host of reasons for my bringing this part of my life up in this book, firstly, it does validate my original premise that I actually did turn out alright, you know like in the so-called 'normal'. Secondly, as stated earlier, my acceptance by, and position in, the medical world, especially in the global cardiovascular communities, allowed me to work side-by-side with many of the world's most educated, talented and skilled cardiologists and cardiovascular surgeons. Not only was I allowed into their clinical world I was also allowed into their personal lives, particularly at international conventions where we would spend days on end attending educational seminars attached at the hip.

More specific to this story I also spent inordinate amounts of time with them in the 'off hours' where they would often 'let their hair down' at which time many of their own idiosyncrasies would, many times unfortunately and unceremoniously, creep out.

One particular night in Nurnberg, Germany, I had taken a number of cardiologists out for dinner where we wined and dined to normal tasteful excess. On the walk back to the hotel one of these ultra-professionals asked if we could take a small detour. He proceeded to explain in a very calm and natural way why he wanted to meander off of the beaten path, it seemed that there was a store close by where he could buy an inflatable cow! I know, I know but we do not want to go there in this family-oriented book. This proclaimed wish to purchase a portable bovine of course inspired another very strange line of conversation in which another of these high-brow cardiologists further enlightened our troupe in the wonderful world of inflatable animals by notifying us that he was aware of twenty-three websites specializing in just inflatable sheep. Oh Boy, what is the so-called 'normal'?

I hate to say it, especially after you have read this book to this point, that in light of the above maybe, just maybe, my childhood upbringing and this entire story wasn't so weird after all!

Somehow or other my rather unorthodox upbringing has left me with an innate ability to always see the glass 'half-full' as opposed to half-empty! In my mind there is almost always humor to be found, even in tragedy.

You may have to look long and hard to find it but, low-and-behold, it will be there somewhere, perhaps hidden by even more tragedy, death or mayhem. Humor is often found in the translations surrounding mayhem. In Germany, even though an authentic 'sense of humor' is a rare find indeed, humorous situations surrounding the misfortunes of others are really not hard to find. The Germans, in fact, have their own word for this exact thing!

I am actually glad to be of German heritage, that's probably where my weird sense of humor comes from. *Schadenfreude* is an actual German word meaning (and *mean* it is!) *satisfaction or pleasure felt at someone else's misfortune*! The word is derived from the German words *schaden* meaning harm and *freude* meaning joy.

A great, if not the greatest example of finding humor in normally devastating circumstances was on the old Mary Tyler Moore TV show. Remember "A little song, a little dance, a little seltzer in your pants"? Surely you haven't forgotten about Chuckles the Clown! Come on now, think, concentrate on the show. Awesome, now do you remember just how Chuckles died?

He actually went out in a big way. Chuckles in fact met his untimely demise as the Grand Marshal in a circus parade where he was dressed as Peter Peanut. During the procession a rogue parade elephant broke loose, grabbed poor Peter and tried to "shell" him, he died from his injuries.

Geez, now that I think about it, maybe there is nothing funny about death: or this whole damned book!

The END is finally here!

ABOUT THE AUTHOR

A.J. MUELLER is a newspaper columnist, an International Cardiovascular and Lithotripsy Consultant, a medical and technical illustrator, an International lecturer on the utilization of Cardiovascular CT in the management of Cardiovascular Disease, a former semi-professional automobile and motorcycle racer, a paid daredevil, a world traveler, general bon vivant and, oh yes, a published author.

His present passions are medical technologies, classic automobiles and writing.

A.J. was born in Hamilton, Ohio, raised in Montreal, Quebec, Canada, was a long-time resident of Florida and now resides in the wonderful but very, very danger-laden Smoky Mountains outside of Murphy, North Carolina.

A.J. can be reached at muellermedical@gmail.co

> *"I am a man, but I can change, if I have to, I think!"*
> Red Green

> *Quando Omni Flunkus, Moritati*
> When all else fails, play dead!
> Possum Lodge Mantra

www.ingramcontent.com/pod-product-compliance
Lightning Source LLC
Chambersburg PA
CBHW060519030426
42337CB00015B/1943